DATE DUE

JAN 1 3 2010

# Careers in Focus

# PHOTOGRAPHY

## SECOND EDITION

Ferguson
*An imprint of Infobase Publishing*

Careers in Focus: Photography, Second Edition

Ferguson
An imprint of Infobase Publishing
132 West 31st Street
New York NY 10001

Library of Congress Cataloging-in-Publication Data

Careers in focus. Photography.—2nd ed.
    p. cm.
Includes bibliographical references and index.
ISBN-13: 978-0-8160-7306-1 (hardcover: alk paper)
ISBN-10: 0-8160-7306-6 (hardcover: alk. paper)
I. Title: Photography.
TR154.C37 2009
770.23—dc22

                                  20090033235

Ferguson books are available at special discounts when purchased in bulk quanti-ties for businesses, associations, institutions, or sales promotions. Please call our Special Sales Department in New York at (212) 967-8800 or (800) 322-8755.

You can find Ferguson on the World Wide Web at http://www.fergpubco.com

Text design by David Strelecky
Cover design by Jooyoung An

Printed in the United States of America

MP MSRF 10 9 8 7 6 5 4 3 2 1

This book is printed on acid-free paper.

# Table of Contents

# Introduction

In 1827, French physicist Joseph Niepce produced the first photograph. In 1829, Niepce went into partnership with Louis Daguerre, who continued to experiment with photography after Niepce's death and ultimately invented what became known as the daguerreotype process. Daguerre reduced the time required to create an image from eight hours to 30 minutes, and he discovered that the resulting image could be made permanent after being immersed in salt.

Daguerre's process, although expensive, became extremely popular. People found it exciting that those without drawing or painting skills could create an image by using a chemical process. The new popularity of photography led to the invention of cheaper and more efficient processes. Soon it was possible to create multiple copies of a photograph, which was something that the daguerreotype process did not allow. In a relatively short period of time, the profession of photography became commercially viable, since many people wanted portraits and other photographs.

Cameras and photo processing have changed dramatically since the time of Niepce and Daguerre. Most cameras manufactured today are battery operated and allow nearly foolproof picture taking by automatically setting shutter speed, lens aperture, and focus. One of the most important developments in photography in recent years is digital photography. Nearly 82 percent of U.S. households own a digital camera, according to Gartner Inc., a market research firm. In digital photography, instead of using film, pictures are recorded on microchips, which can then be downloaded onto a computer's hard drive. They can be manipulated in size, color, and shape, virtually eliminating the need for a darkroom.

Photographs are also being combined with other media in new ways, and it is likely that this trend will continue. The Internet is a new arena for photographers and other artists. Web sites like Flickr and Facebook allow amateur photographers to showcase their work to a worldwide audience. New technology makes it possible to broadcast full-length features on the Internet, and photographers and cinematographers will have to both adapt their existing techniques and find new ones in order to use the Internet effectively. Because of these new technologies, today's professional photographers and related workers are employed in many industries, including advertising, fine art, film, television, food, fashion, library science, medical science, education, journalism, museums and cultural centers, publishing, and sports.

According to the *Occupational Outlook Handbook,* employment of photographers is expected to grow as fast as the average for all occupations over the next several years. The demand for photographs is expected to increase during that period, but the business of photography is now and will remain extremely competitive. There are far more people who want to be photographers than there are positions available. Only those individuals with the best skills, training, and business acumen are likely to succeed in the field as salaried workers or independent contractors.

Photography students need to study digital processes or they will be at a disadvantage in the job market when they graduate. Study of traditional photography is still recommended, but because film-based photographs are commonly scanned, it is also necessary to study digital photography.

The newspaper industry is expected to decline, which will affect jobs for print photographers. There should be jobs available for photographers in news and wire services, particularly those who are knowledgeable in digital processes. Digital images will also be in demand by book, magazine, and journal publishers, and Internet businesses.

Employment growth is expected to be slow for photographic equipment repairers and photo processing workers due to the move toward digital processes.

The articles in *Careers in Focus: Photography* appear in Ferguson's *Encyclopedia of Careers and Vocational Guidance,* but have been updated and revised with the latest information from the U.S. Department of Labor, professional organizations, and other sources.

The following paragraphs detail the sections and features that appear in the book.

The **Quick Facts** section provides a brief summary of the career including recommended school subjects, personal skills, work environment, minimum educational requirements, salary ranges, certification or licensing requirements, and employment outlook. This section also provides acronyms and identification numbers for the following government classification indexes: the *Dictionary of Occupational Titles* (DOT), the *Guide for Occupational Exploration* (GOE), the National Occupational Classification (NOC) Index, and the Occupational Information Network (O*NET)-Standard Occupational Classification System (SOC) index. The DOT, GOE, and O*NET-SOC indexes have been created by the U.S. government; the NOC index is Canada's career classification system. Readers can use the identification numbers listed in the Quick Facts section to access further information about a career. Print editions of the DOT (*Dictionary of Occupational Titles.* Indianapolis, Ind.: JIST Works, 1991) and GOE (*Guide for Occupational Exploration.* Indianapolis, Ind.: JIST Works, 2001) are available at libraries. Electronic versions of the NOC (http://www23.hrdc-drhc.gc.ca) and O*NET-SOC (http://online.onetcenter.org) are available on the Internet. When no DOT, GOE, NOC, or O*NET-SOC numbers are present, this means that the U.S. Department of Labor or Human Resources Development Canada have not created a numerical designation for this career. In this instance, you will see the acronym "N/A," or not available.

The **Overview** section is a brief introductory description of the duties and responsibilities involved in this career. Oftentimes, a career may have a variety of job titles. When this is the case, alternative career titles are presented. Employment statistics are also provided, when available. The **History** section describes the history of the particular job as it relates to the overall development of its industry or field. **The Job** describes the primary and secondary duties of the job. **Requirements** discusses high school and postsecondary education and training requirements, any certification or licensing that is necessary, and other personal requirements for success in the job. **Exploring** offers suggestions on how to gain experience in or knowledge of the particular job before making a firm educational and financial commitment. The focus is on what can be done while still in high school (or in the early years of college) to gain a better understanding of the job. The **Employers** section gives an overview of typical places of employment for the job. **Starting Out** discusses the best ways to land that first job, be it through the college career services office, newspaper ads, Internet employment sites, or personal contact. The **Advancement** section describes what kind of career path to expect from the job and how to get there. **Earnings** lists salary ranges and describes the typical fringe benefits. The **Work Environment** section describes the typical surroundings and conditions of employment—whether indoors or outdoors, noisy or quiet, social or independent. Also discussed are typical hours worked, any seasonal fluctuations, and the stresses and strains of the job. The **Outlook** section summarizes the job in terms of the general economy and industry projections. For the most part, Outlook information is obtained from the U.S. Bureau of Labor Statistics and is supplemented by information gathered from professional associations. Job growth terms follow those used in the *Occupational Outlook Handbook.* Growth described as "much faster than the average" means an increase of 21 percent or more. Growth described as "faster than the average" means an increase of 14 to 20 percent. Growth described as "about as fast as the average" means an increase of 7 to 13 percent. Growth described as "more slowly than the average" means an increase of 3 to 6 percent. "Little or no change" means a decrease of 2 percent to an increase of 2 percent. "Decline" means a decrease of 3 percent or more. Each article ends with **For More Information,** which lists organizations that provide information on training, education, internships, scholarships, and job placement.

*Careers in Focus: Photography* also includes photos, informative sidebars, and interviews with professionals in the field.

If you have a good eye for photography and already enjoy taking pictures as a hobby, there might be a rewarding career in photography in store for you. Take the time to investigate the different photography careers described in this book, and contact the various organizations for more information.

# Archivists

## OVERVIEW

*Archivists* contribute to the study of the arts and sciences by analyzing, acquiring, and preserving historical documents, artwork, organizational and personal records, and information systems that are significant enough to be preserved for future generations. Archivists keep track of artifacts such as photographs, films, video and sound recordings, letters, contracts, blueprints, electronic information, and other items of potential historical significance. Approximately 27,000 archivists, curators, and museum technicians are employed in the United States.

## HISTORY

For centuries, archives have served as repositories for the official records of governments, educational institutions, businesses, religious organizations, families, and countless other groups. From the first time information was recorded, there has been a need to preserve those accounts. The evolution of archiving information in a manner similar to what we know today can be traced back to the Middle Ages.

As the feudal system in Europe gave way to nations with systematic and complex legal systems, precise record keeping was needed to keep track of land ownership and official policy. These records helped governments serve the needs of their nations and protected the rights of the common people in civil matters.

In America, early settlers maintained records using skills they brought from their European homelands. Families kept records of the journey to their new country and saved correspondence with family members still in Europe. Religious institutions kept records

## QUICK FACTS

**School Subjects**
English
Foreign language
History

**Personal Skills**
Communication/ideas
Leadership/management

**Work Environment**
Primarily indoors
Primarily one location

**Minimum Education Level**
Master's degree

**Salary Range**
$26,330 to $43,110 to $73,050+

**Certification or Licensing**
Voluntary

**Outlook**
Faster than the average

**DOT**
101

**GOE**
12.03.04

**NOC**
5113

**O*NET-SOC**
25-4011.00

of the births, deaths, and marriages of their members. Settlers kept track of their business transactions, such as land purchases, crop trades, and building constructions.

In the early 18th century, similar to what occurred in Europe in the Middle Ages, civic records in America became more prevalent as towns became incorporated. Leaders needed to maintain accurate records of property ownership and laws made by—and for—citizens.

Although archives have been incorporated in one form or another for centuries, archivists have established themselves as professionals only in the last century or so. In the past, museums and societies accumulated records and objects rapidly and sometimes indiscriminately, accepting items regardless of their actual merit. Each archive had its own system of documenting, organizing, and storing materials. In 1884, the American Historical Association was formed to develop archival standards and help boost interaction among archivists.

Each year, as new scientific discoveries are made and new works are published, the need for sifting through and classifying items increases. More advanced computer systems will help archivists catalog archival materials as well as make archives more readily available to users. Advances in conservation techniques will help extend the life of fragile items, allowing them to be available to future generations.

## THE JOB

Archivists analyze documents and materials such as historical photographs, government records, minutes of corporate board meetings, letters from famous people, charters of nonprofit foundations, maps, coins, works of art, and nearly anything else that may have historical significance. To determine which documents should be saved, they consider such factors as when the resource was created, who created it, and for whom it was created. In deciding on other items to archive, the archivist needs to consider the provenance, or history of creation and ownership, of the materials. They also take into account the physical capacity of their employer's archives. For instance, a repository with very little space for new materials may need to decline the gift of a large or bulky item, despite its potential value.

Various organizations, including government agencies, corporations, universities, and museums, maintain archives, and the value of documents is generally dictated by whichever group owns them. For example, the U.S. Army may not be interested in a photo archive of the work of American photographers of the early 20th century, and a university archives may not be interested in a Civil War battle plan. Archivists understand and serve the needs of their employers and collect items that are most relevant to their organizations.

Archivists may also be in charge of collecting items of historical significance to the institution for which they work. An archivist at a university, for instance, may collect new copies of the student newspaper to keep historical documentation of student activities and issues up to date or old photographs and movies of student activities, clubs, or sporting events. An archivist at a public library may prepare, present, and store annual reports of the branch libraries in order to keep an accurate record of library statistics.

After selecting appropriate materials, archivists make them accessible to others by preparing reference aids such as indexes, guides, bibliographies, descriptions, and microfilmed copies and slides of documents and photographs. These research aids may be printed up and kept in the organization's stack area, put online so off-site researchers have access to the information, or put on CD-ROM for distribution to other individuals or organizations. Archivists also file and cross-index archived items for easy retrieval when a user wishes to consult a collection.

Archivists may preserve and repair historical documents or send damaged items to a professional conservator. They may also appraise the items based on their knowledge of political, economic, military, and social history, as well as by the materials' physical condition, research potential, and rarity.

Many archivists conduct research using the archival materials at their disposal, and they may publish articles detailing their findings. They may advise government agencies, scholars, journalists, and others conducting research by supplying available materials and information. Archivists also act as reference contacts and teachers. An employee doing research at the company archives may have little knowledge of how and where to begin. The archivist may suggest the worker consult specific reference guides or browse through an online catalog. After the employee decides which materials will be of most use, the archivist may retrieve the archives from storage, circulate the collection to the user, and perhaps even instruct the user as to the proper handling of fragile or oversize materials.

Archivists may have assistants who help them with the sorting and indexing of archival collections. At a university library, undergraduate or graduate students usually act as archival assistants. Small community historical societies may rely on trained volunteers to assist the archivist.

Depending on the size of their employing organization, archivists may perform many or few administrative duties. Such duties may include preparing budgets, representing their institutions at scientific or association conferences, soliciting support for institutions, and interviewing and hiring personnel. Some help formulate and interpret institutional policy. In addition, archivists may plan or participate in special research projects and write articles for scientific journals.

It is important to note that many positions in archival management are on a temporary or contract basis, as archivists are often hired to process a specific collection. When the processing is finished, so may be the archivist's employment. The timeline of such contracts may span several months to several years, and some positions do become permanent.

## REQUIREMENTS

### High School

If you are interested in doing archival work, high school is not too early to begin your training. Since it is usually necessary to earn a master's degree to become an archivist, you should select a college preparatory curriculum in high school and plan on going to college. While in high school, sharpen your library and research skills. Classes in English, history, science, and mathematics will provide you with basic skills and knowledge for university study. Journalism courses will hone your research skills, and political science courses will help you identify events of societal importance. You should also plan on learning at least one foreign language. If you are interested in doing archival work at a religious organization, Latin or Hebrew may be good language options. If you would like to work in a specialized archive, such as an art gallery or medical school archive, you should also focus on classes that will prepare you for that specialty.

### Postsecondary Training

To prepare for archival work in college, you should get a degree in the liberal arts. You will probably want to study history, library science, or a related field, since there are currently no undergraduate programs that deal solely with the archival sciences. You should take any specific courses in archival methods that are available to you as an undergraduate. Since many employers prefer to hire archivists with a graduate degree, consider any course load that may help you gain entrance into a program to earn a master's degree in library and information science or history.

Graduate school will give you the opportunity to learn more specific details about archival work. More than 65 colleges and universities offer classes in the archival sciences as part of other degree programs. These courses will teach you about many aspects of archival work, from selecting items and organizing collections to preparing documentation and conserving materials.

While in graduate school, you may be able to secure a part-time job or assistantship at your school's archives. Many university archives rely on their own students to provide valuable help maintaining collections, and students who work there gain firsthand knowledge and experience in the archival field.

Many positions require a second master's degree in a specific field or a doctorate degree. An archivist at a historical society may need a master's degree in history and another master's in library and information science. Candidates with bachelor's degrees may serve as assistants while they complete their formal training.

### Certification or Licensing

Although not currently required by most employers, voluntary certification for archivists is available from the Academy of Certified Archivists. Certification is earned by gaining practical experience in archival work, taking requisite courses, and passing an examination on the history, theory, and practice of archival science. Archivists need to renew their certification status every five years, usually by examination. Certification can be especially useful to archivists wishing to work in the corporate world.

### Other Requirements

Archivists need to have excellent research and organizational skills. They should be comfortable working with rare and fragile materials. They need to maintain archives with absolute discretion, especially in the case of closed archives or archives available only for specific users. Archivists also need to be able to communicate effectively with all types of people that may use the archives, since they will be explaining the research methods and the policies and procedures of their organization. Finally, archivists may be required to move heavy boxes and other awkward materials. An archivist should be comfortable lifting or carrying large objects, although requirements may be different for various organizations and arrangements can often be made for professionals with different abilities.

## EXPLORING

If you are interested in archival work, a good way to learn about the field is by using archives for your own research. Visit the archives of a local college or university to learn about that institution's history and some of its notable graduates. A visit to the archives of a candy manufacturer could help you with an assignment on the history of a specific type of production method. Since institutions may limit access to their collections, be sure to contact the organization about your project before you make the trip.

Getting to know an archivist can give you a good perspective of the field and the specific duties of the professional archivist. You could also see if a professional archival or historical association offers special student memberships or mentoring opportunities.

You can also learn more about archival work by creating your own family archive consisting of letters, birth and marriage certificates, old photographs, special awards, and any other documents that would help someone understand your family's history.

Another way to gain practical experience is to obtain part-time or volunteer positions in archives, historical societies, or libraries. Many museums and cultural centers train volunteer guides (called *docents*) to give tours of their institutions. If you already volunteer for an organization in another capacity, ask to have a personal tour of the archives.

## EMPLOYERS

Archivists can find employment in various fields. Nearly one-third of the nation's archivists are employed in government positions, working for the Department of Defense, the National Archives and Records Administration, and other local, state, and federal repositories. Approximately 18 percent of archivists work in academia, working in college and university libraries. Other archivists work in positions for museums, historical societies, and zoos.

Archivists are also on staff at corporations, religious institutions, and professional associations. Many of these organizations need archivists to manage massive amounts of records that will be kept for posterity, or to comply with state or federal regulations. Some private collectors may also employ an archivist to process, organize, and catalog their personal holdings.

## STARTING OUT

There is no best way to become an archivist. Since there is no formal archivist degree, many people working in the field today have had to pave their own way. Daniel Meyer, associate curator of special collections and university archivist at the University of Chicago Library, began by earning a master's degree in history and then a Ph.D. In graduate school, he processed collections in his university's archives.

By enhancing his educational credentials with practical experience in the field, he gradually moved on to positions with greater degrees of responsibility.

Another archivist may approach his or her career from another direction. For example, an archivist could start out with a master's degree in French and then earn a master's of library science (M.L.S.) degree, with a concentration in archival management. With a language background and the M.L.S., he or she could begin working in archival positions in colleges and universities. Candidates for positions as archivists should apply to institutions for entry-level positions only after completing their undergraduate degrees—usually in history. An archivist going into a particular area of archival work, however, may wish to earn a degree in that field. If you are interested in working in a museum's archives, for instance, you may wish to pursue a degree in art or photography.

Many potential archivists choose to work part time as research assistants, interns, or volunteers in order to gain archival experience. Gaining hands-on experience in archival management through an internship or student employment is essential for finding employment as an archivist. School career services offices are good starting points to look for research assistantships and internships. Professional librarian and archivist associations often have job listings for those new to the field.

## ADVANCEMENT

Archivists usually work in small sections, units, or departments, so internal promotion opportunities are often limited. Promising archivists advance by gaining more responsibility for the administration of the collections. They may begin to spend more time supervising the work of others. Archivists can also advance by transferring to larger repositories and taking more administration-based positions.

Because the best jobs as archivists are contingent upon education, the surest method of advancement is through pursuing advanced or specialized degrees. Archivists should also attend conferences and workshops to stay current with developments in their fields. Archivists can enhance their status by conducting independent research and publishing their findings. In a public or private library, an archivist may move on to a position such as curator, chief librarian, or library director.

Archivists may also move outside of the standard archival field entirely. With their background and skills, archivists may become teachers, university professors, or instructors at a library school.

They may also set up shop for themselves as archival consultants to corporations or private collectors.

## EARNINGS

Salaries for archivists vary considerably by institution and may depend on education and experience. People employed by the federal government or by prestigious museums generally earn more than those working for small organizations. The U.S. Department of Labor reported that the mean annual salary for archivists working for the federal government was $74,730 in 2007. Those working in museums or historical sites earned a mean salary of $40,060. The median salary for all archivists was $43,110. The lowest paid 10 percent earned $26,330 or less, while the highest paid 10 percent earned $73,050 or more.

Archivists who work for large corporations, institutions, or government agencies generally receive a full range of benefits, including health care coverage, vacation days, paid holidays, paid sick time, and retirement savings plans. Self-employed archival consultants usually have to provide their own benefits. All archivists have the added benefit of working with rare and unique materials. They have the opportunity to work with history and create documentation of the past.

## WORK ENVIRONMENT

Because dirt, sunlight, and moisture can damage materials and documents, archivists generally work in clean, climate-controlled surroundings with artificial lighting rather than windows. Many archives are small offices, often employing the archivist alone, or with one or two part-time volunteers. Other archives are part of a larger department within an organization. The archives for DePaul University in Chicago, for instance, are part of the special collections department and are managed by the curator. With this type of arrangement, the archivist generally has a number of graduate assistants to help with the processing of materials and departmental support staff to assist with clerical tasks.

Archivist positions usually involve little physical activity, save for the bending, lifting, and reaching they may need to do in order to arrange collections and make room for new materials. Also, some archival collections include not only paper records but some over-sized items as well. The archives of an elite fraternal organization, for example, may house a collection of hats or uniforms that members wore throughout the years, each of which must be processed, cataloged, preserved, and stored.

Most archivists work 40 hours per week, usually during regular, weekday working hours. Depending on the needs of their department and the community they serve, an archive may be open some weekend hours, thus requiring the archivist to be on hand for users. Also, archivists spend some of their time traveling to the homes of donors to view materials that may complement an archival collection.

## OUTLOOK

Job opportunities for archivists are expected to increase faster than the average for all careers through 2016, according to the U.S. Department of Labor. But since qualified job applicants outnumber the positions available, competition for jobs as archivists is keen. Candidates with specialized training, such as master's degrees in history and library science and a concentration in archives or record management, will have better opportunities. A doctorate in history or a related field can also be a boon to job-seeking archivists. Graduates who have studied archival work or records management will be in higher demand than those without that background. Also, by gaining related work or volunteer experience, many potential archivists will be in a better position to find full-time employment. As archival work begins to reflect an increasingly digital society, an archivist with extensive knowledge of computers is likely to advance more quickly than an archivist with little desire to learn. Archivists who specialize in electronic records and records management will have the best employment prospects.

Jobs are expected to increase as more corporations and private organizations establish an archival history. Archivists will also be needed to fill positions left vacant by retirees and archivists who leave the occupation. On the other hand, budget cuts in educational institutions, museums, and cultural institutions often reduce demand for archivists. Overall, there will always be positions available for archivists, but the aspiring archivist may need to be creative, flexible, and determined in forging a career path.

## FOR MORE INFORMATION

*To find out about archival certification procedures, contact*
**Academy of Certified Archivists**
90 State Street, Suite 1009
Albany, NY 12207-1710

Tel: 518-463-8644
Email: aca@caphill.com
http://www.certifiedarchivists.org

*For information about archival programs, activities, and publications in North America, contact*
**American Institute for Conservation of Historic and Artistic Works**
1156 15th Street, NW, Suite 320
Washington, DC 20005-1714
Tel: 202-452-9545
Email: info@aic-faic.org
http://aic.stanford.edu

*If you are interested in working with the archives of film and television, contact*
**Association of Moving Image Archivists**
1313 North Vine Street
Hollywood, CA 90028-8107
Tel: 323-463-1500
Email: amia@amianet.org
http://amianet.org

*For information on archivists who are employed by government agencies, contact*
**National Association of Government Archives and Records Administrators**
90 State Street, Suite 1009
Albany, NY 12207-1710
Tel: 518-463-8644
Email: nagara@caphill.com
http://www.nagara.org

*For a list of educational programs and to read* So You Want to Be an Archivist: An Overview of the Archival Profession, *visit the SAA Web site.*
**Society of American Archivists (SAA)**
17 North State Street, Suite 1425
Chicago, IL 60602-3315
Tel: 866-722-7858
Email: info@archivists.org
http://www.archivists.org

# Art Directors

## OVERVIEW

*Art directors* play a key role in every stage of the creation of an advertisement or ad campaign, from formulating concepts to supervising production. Ultimately, they are responsible for planning and overseeing the presentation of their clients' messages in print or on screen—that is, in books, magazines, newspapers, television commercials, posters, and packaging, as well as in film and video and on the Internet.

In publishing, art directors work with artists, photographers, and text editors to develop visual images and generate copy, according to the marketing strategy. They evaluate existing illustrations, determine presentation styles and techniques, hire both staff and freelance talent, work with layouts, and prepare budgets.

In films, videos, and television commercials, art directors set the general look of the visual elements and approve the props, costumes, and models. In addition, they are involved in casting, editing, and selecting the music. In film (motion pictures) and video, the art director is usually an experienced animator or computer/graphic arts designer who supervises animators or other artistic staff.

In sum, art directors are charged with selling to, informing, and educating consumers. They supervise both in-house and off-site staff, handle executive issues, and oversee the entire artistic production process. There are approximately 78,000 art directors working in the United States.

## HISTORY

Artists have always been an important part of the creative process. Medieval monks illuminated their manuscripts, painting with egg-white tempera on vellum. Each copy of each book had to be printed and illustrated individually.

Printed illustrations first appeared in books in 1461. Through the years, prints were made through woodblock, copperplate, lithography, and other means of duplicating images. Although making many copies of the same illustration was possible, publishers still depended on individual artists to create the original works. Text editors usually decided what was to be illustrated and how, while artists commonly supervised the production of the artwork.

The first art directors were probably staff illustrators for book publishers. As the publishing industry grew more complex and incorporated new technologies such as photography and film, art direction evolved into a more supervisory position and became a full-time job. Publishers and advertisers began to need specialists who could acquire and use illustrations and photos. Women's magazines, such as *Vogue* (http://www.style.com/vogue) and *Harper's Bazaar* (http://www.harpersbazaar.com), and photo magazines, such as *National Geographic* (http://www.nationalgeographic.com), relied so much on illustration and photography that the photo editor and art director began to carry as much power as the text editor.

With the creation of animation, art directors became more indispensable than ever. Animated short films, such as the early Mickey Mouse cartoons, were usually supervised by art directors. Walt Disney was the art director on many of his early pictures. In full-length animated feature films, the sheer number of illustrations requires more than one art director to oversee the project.

Today's art directors supervise almost every type of visual project produced. Through a variety of methods and media, from television and film to magazines, comic books, and the Internet, art directors communicate ideas by selecting and supervising every element that goes into the finished product.

## THE JOB

Art directors are responsible for all visual aspects of printed or on-screen projects. The art director oversees the process of developing visual solutions to a variety of communication problems. He or she helps to establish corporate identities; advertises products and services; enhances books, magazines, newsletters, and other publications; and creates television commercials, film and video productions, and Web sites. Some art directors with experience or knowledge in specific fields specialize in such areas as packaging, exhibitions and displays, or the Internet. But all directors, even those with specialized backgrounds, must be skilled in and knowledgeable about design, illustration, photography, computers, research, and writing in order to supervise the work of graphic artists, photographers, copywriters, text editors, and other employees.

In print advertising and publishing, art directors may begin with the client's concept or develop one in collaboration with the copywriter and account executive. Once the concept is established, the next step is to decide on the most effective way to communicate it. If there is text, for example, should the art director choose illustrations based on specific text references, or should the illustrations fill in the gaps in the copy? If a piece is being revised, existing illustrations must be reevaluated.

After deciding what needs to be illustrated, art directors must find sources that can create or provide the art. Photo agencies, for example, have photographs and illustrations on thousands of different subjects. If, however, the desired illustration does not exist, it may have to be commissioned or designed by one of the staff designers. Commissioning artwork means that the art director contacts a photographer or illustrator and explains what is needed. A price is negotiated, and the artist creates the image specifically for the art director.

Once the illustrations and other art elements have been secured, they must be presented in an appealing manner. The art director supervises (and may help in the production of) the layout of the piece and presents the final version to the client or creative director. Layout is the process of figuring out where every image, headline, and block of text will be placed on the page. The size, style, and method of reproduction must all be specifically indicated so that the image is recreated as the director intended it.

In broadcast advertising and film and video, the art director has a wide variety of responsibilities and often interacts with an enormous number of creative professionals. Working with directors and producers, art directors interpret scripts and create or select settings in order to visually convey the story or the message. The art director oversees set decorators and designers, model makers, location managers, propmasters, construction coordinators, and special effects people. In addition, art directors work with writers, unit production managers, cinematographers, costume designers, and post-production staff, including editors and employees responsible for scoring and titles. The art director is ultimately responsible for all visual aspects of the finished product.

The process of producing a television commercial begins in much the same way that a printed advertising piece is created. The art director may start with the client's concept or create one in-house in collaboration with staff members. Once a concept has been created and the copywriter has generated the corresponding text, the art director sketches a rough storyboard based on the writer's ideas, and the plan is presented for review to the creative director. The next step is to develop a finished storyboard, with larger and more detailed frames (the individual scenes) in color. This storyboard is presented to the client for review and used as a guide for the film director as well.

Technology has been playing an increasingly important role in the art director's job. Most art directors, for example, use a variety of computer software programs, including Adobe InDesign, Frame-Maker, Illustrator, and Photoshop, and Dreamweaver; QuarkX-Press; and CorelDRAW. Many others create and oversee Web sites for clients and work with other interactive media and materials, including CD-ROM, touch-screens, multidimensional visuals, and new animation programs.

Art directors usually work on more than one project at a time and must be able to keep numerous, unrelated details straight. They often work under pressure of a deadline and yet must remain calm and pleasant when dealing with clients and staff. Because they are supervisors, art directors are often called upon to resolve problems, not only with projects but with employees as well.

Art directors are not entry-level workers. They usually have years of experience working at lower-level jobs in the field before gaining the knowledge needed to supervise projects. Depending on whether they work primarily in publishing or film, art directors have to know how printing presses operate or how film is processed. They should also be familiar with a variety of production techniques in order to understand the wide range of ways that images can be manipulated to meet the needs of a project.

## REQUIREMENTS

### High School

A college degree is usually a requirement for art directors; however, in some instances it is not absolutely necessary. A variety of high school courses will give you both a taste of college-level offerings and an idea of the skills necessary for art directors on the job. These courses include art, drawing, art history, graphic design, illustration, photography, advertising, and desktop publishing.

Math courses are also important. Most of the elements of sizing an image involve calculating percentage reduction or enlargement of the original picture. This must be done with a great degree of accuracy if the overall design is going to work. For example, type size may have to be figured within a thirty-second of an inch for a print project. Errors can be extremely costly and may make the project look sloppy.

Other useful courses that you should take in high school include business, computing, English, technical drawing, cultural studies, psychology, and social science.

## Postsecondary Training

According to the American Institute of Graphic Arts, nine out of 10 artists have a college degree. Among them, six out of 10 have majored in graphic design, and two out of 10 have majored in fine arts. In addition, almost two out of 10 have a master's degree. Along with general two- and four-year colleges and universities, a number of professional art schools offer two-, three-, or four-year programs with such classes as figure drawing, painting, graphic design, and other art courses, as well as classes in art history, writing, business administration, communications, and foreign languages.

Courses in advertising, marketing, photography, filmmaking, set direction, layout, desktop publishing, and fashion are also important for those interested in becoming art directors. Specialized courses, sometimes offered only at professional art schools, may be particularly helpful for students who want to go into art direction. These include typography, animation, storyboard, Web site design, and portfolio development.

Because of the rapidly increasing use of computers in design work, it is essential to have a thorough understanding of how computer art and layout programs work. In smaller companies, the art director may be responsible for operating this equipment; in larger companies, a staff person, under the direction of the art director, may use these programs. In either case, the director must know what can be done with the available equipment.

In addition to course work at the college level, many universities and professional art schools offer graduates or students in their final year a variety of workshop projects, desktop publishing training opportunities, and internships. These programs provide students with opportunities to develop their personal design styles and portfolios.

## Other Requirements

The work of an art director requires creativity, imagination, curiosity, and a sense of adventure. Art directors must be able to work with all sorts of specialized equipment and computer software, such as graphic design programs, as well as make presentations on the ideas behind their work.

The ability to work well with different people and organizations is a must for art directors. They must always be up to date on new techniques, trends, and attitudes. And because deadlines are a constant part of the work, an ability to handle stress and pressure well is key.

Accuracy and attention to detail are important parts of the job. When art is done neatly and correctly, the public usually pays no notice. But when a project is done poorly or sloppily, people will notice, even if they have had no design training. Other requirements for art directors include time management skills and an interest in media and people's motivations and lifestyles.

## EXPLORING

High school students can get an idea of what an art director does by working on the staff of the school newspaper, magazine, or yearbook, and developing their own Web sites or zines. It may also be possible to secure a part-time job assisting the advertising director of the local newspaper or to work at an advertising agency. Developing your own artistic talent is important, and this can be accomplished through self-training (reading books and practicing) or through courses in painting, drawing, or other creative arts. At the very least, you should develop your "creative eye," that is, your ability to develop ideas visually. One way to do this is by familiarizing yourself with great works, such as paintings or highly creative magazine ads, motion pictures, videos, or commercials.

Students can also become members of a variety of art or advertising clubs around the nation. If you have access to the Internet, check out Paleta: The Art Project (http://www.paletaworld.org) to join a free art club. In addition to keeping members up to date on industry trends, such clubs offer job information, resources, and a variety of other benefits.

## EMPLOYERS

Approximately 78,000 art directors are employed in the United States. A variety of organizations in virtually all industries employ art directors. They might work at advertising agencies, publishing houses, museums, packaging firms, photography studios, marketing and public relations firms, desktop publishing outfits, digital prepress houses, or printing companies. Art directors who oversee and produce on-screen products often work for film production houses, Web designers, multimedia developers, computer games developers, or television stations.

While companies of all sizes employ art directors, smaller organizations often combine the positions of graphic designer, illustrator, and art director. And although opportunities for art direction can be found all across the nation and abroad, many larger firms in such cities as Chicago, New York, and Los Angeles usually have more openings, as well as higher pay scales, than smaller companies.

## STARTING OUT

Since an art director's job requires a great deal of experience, it is usually not considered an entry-level position. Typically, a person on a career track toward art director is hired as an assistant to an established director. Recent graduates wishing to enter advertising should have a portfolio of their work containing seven to 10 sample ads to demonstrate their understanding of both the business and the media in which they want to work.

Serving as an intern is a good way to get experience and develop skills. Graduates should also consider taking an entry-level job in a publisher's art department to gain initial experience. Either way, aspiring art directors must be willing to acquire their credentials by working on various projects. This may mean working in a variety of areas, such as advertising, marketing, editing, and design.

College publications offer students a chance to gain experience and develop portfolios. In addition, many students are able to do freelance work while still in school, allowing them to make important industry contacts and gain on-the-job experience at the same time.

## ADVANCEMENT

While some may be content to remain an art director upon reaching that position, many art directors take on even more responsibility within their organizations, become television directors, start their own advertising agencies, create their own Web sites, develop original multimedia programs, or launch their own magazines.

Many people who get to the position of art director do not advance beyond the title but move on to work at more prestigious firms. Competition for positions at companies that have national reputations continues to be keen because of the sheer number of talented people interested. At smaller publications or local companies, the competition may be less intense, since candidates are competing primarily against others in the local market.

| Earnings for Art Directors by Industry, 2007 | |
| --- | --- |
| Field | Mean Annual Earnings |
| Management of Companies and Enterprises | $97,070 |
| Specialized Design Services | $96,460 |
| Motion Picture and Video Industries | $90,000 |
| Advertising and Related Services | $87,970 |
| Newspaper, Periodical, Book, and Directory Publishers | $71,020 |

Source: U.S. Department of Labor

## EARNINGS

The job title of art director can mean many different things, depending on the company at which the director is employed. According to the U.S. Department of Labor, a beginning art director or an art director who worked at a small firm earned $39,600 or less per year in 2007, while experienced art directors working at larger companies earned more than $144,380. Mean annual earnings for art directors employed in the advertising industry (the largest employer of salaried art directors) were $87,970 in 2007. The median annual earnings for art directors working in all industries were $72,320. (Again, it is important to note that these positions are not entry level; beginning art directors have probably already accumulated several years of experience in the field for which they were paid far less.)

According to the American Institute of Graphic Arts' Aquent Salary Survey 2007, the median salary for art directors was $70,000. Art directors in the 25th percentile earned $55,000 annually, while those in the 75th percentile made $82,000 per year. Salaries varied by geographic region. For example, art directors in the Mid-Atlantic states had average salaries of $75,000 a year, while those in the Mountain region earned an average of $55,000.

Most companies employing art directors offer insurance benefits, a retirement plan, and other incentives and bonuses.

## WORK ENVIRONMENT

Art directors usually work in studios or office buildings. While their work areas are comfortable, well lit, and ventilated, they often handle glue, paint, ink, and other materials that pose safety hazards, and they should, therefore, exercise caution.

Art directors at art and design studios and publishing firms usually work a standard 40-hour week. Many, however, work overtime during busy periods in order to meet deadlines. Similarly, directors at film and video operations and at television studios work as many hours as required—usually many more than 40 per week—in order to finish projects according to predetermined schedules.

While art directors work independently while reviewing artwork and reading copy, much of their time is spent collaborating with and supervising a team of employees, often consisting of copywriters, editors, photographers, graphic artists, and account executives.

## OUTLOOK

The extent to which art director positions are in demand, like many other positions, depends on the economy in general; when times are tough, people and businesses spend less, and cutbacks are made. When the economy is healthy, employment prospects for art directors will be favorable. The U.S. Department of Labor predicts that employment for art directors will grow about as fast as the average for all occupations through 2016. One area that shows particularly good promise for growth is the retail industry, since more and more large retail establishments, especially catalog houses, will be employing in-house advertising art directors.

In addition, producers of all kinds of products continually need advertisers to reach their potential customers, and publishers always want some type of illustration to enhance their books and magazines. Creators of films and videos also need images in order to produce their programs, and people working with new media are increasingly looking for artists and directors to promote new and existing products and services, enhance their Web sites, develop new multimedia programs, and create multidimensional visuals. People who can quickly and creatively generate new concepts and ideas will be in high demand.

However, it is important to note that the supply of aspiring artists is expected to exceed the number of job openings. As a result, those wishing to enter the field will encounter keen competition for salaried, staff positions as well as for freelance work. And although the Internet is expected to provide many opportunities for artists and art directors, some firms are hiring employees without formal art or design training to operate computer-aided design systems and oversee work.

## FOR MORE INFORMATION

*The AAF is the professional advertising association that binds the mutual interests of corporate advertisers, agencies, media companies, suppliers, and academia. For more information, contact*
**American Advertising Federation (AAF)**
1101 Vermont Avenue, NW, Suite 500
Washington, DC 20005-6306
Tel: 800-999-2231
Email: aaf@aaf.org
http://www.aaf.org

*This management-oriented national trade organization represents the advertising agency business. For information, contact*
**American Association of Advertising Agencies**
405 Lexington Avenue, 18th Floor
New York, NY 10174-1801
Tel: 212-682-2500
http://www.aaaa.org

*For more information on design professionals, contact*
**American Institute of Graphic Arts**
164 Fifth Avenue
New York, NY 10010-5901
Tel: 212-807-1990
http://www.aiga.org

*The Art Directors Club is an international, nonprofit organization of directors in advertising, graphic design, interactive media, broadcast design, typography, packaging, environmental design, photography, illustration, and related disciplines. For information, contact*
**Art Directors Club**
106 West 29th Street
New York, NY 10001-5301
Tel: 212-643-1440
Email: info@adcglobal.org
http://www.adcglobal.org

*For information on the graphic arts, contact*
**Graphic Artists Guild**
32 Broadway, Suite 1114
New York, NY 10004-1612
Tel: 212-791-3400
http://www.gag.org

# Camera Operators

## OVERVIEW

*Camera operators* use motion picture cameras and equipment to photograph subjects or material for movies, television programs, or commercials. They usually use 35-millimeter or 16-millimeter cameras or camcorders and a variety of films, lenses, tripods, and filters in their work. Their instructions usually come from cinematographers or directors of photography. Approximately 27,000 camera operators work in the United States.

## HISTORY

Motion pictures were made as early as 1877, using a series of still photographs to create the illusion of motion. But it was Thomas Edison who, in 1889, produced the first single-unit motion picture camera that set the standard for today.

The motion picture industry blossomed in the United States during the 20th century. With the growth of the television industry and the addition of commercial advertising to television, camera operators became indispensable members of the production crew. Motion picture directors and producers rely on camera operators to create the images on film that the directors and producers envision in their minds. As camera equipment becomes more complex and sophisticated, the camera operator will need to be more proficient at his or her craft.

## QUICK FACTS

**School Subjects**
Art
Mathematics

**Personal Skills**
Communication/ideas
Mechanical/manipulative

**Work Environment**
Indoors and outdoors
Primarily multiple locations

**Minimum Education Level**
High school diploma

**Salary Range**
$21,050 to $41,850 to $78,330+

**Certification or Licensing**
None available

**Outlook**
About as fast as the average

**DOT**
143

**GOE**
01.08.01

**NOC**
5222

**O*NET-SOC**
27-4031.00

## THE JOB

Motion picture camera operators may work on feature films in Hollywood or on location elsewhere. Many work on educational films, documentaries, or television programs. The nature of the camera operator's work depends largely on the size of the production crew. If the film is a documentary or short news segment, the camera operator may be responsible for setting up the camera and lighting equipment as well as for supervising the actors during filming. Equipment that camera operators typically use include cranes, dollies, mounting heads, and different types of lenses and accessories. Often the camera operator is also responsible for maintenance and repair of all of this equipment.

With a larger crew, the camera operator is responsible only for the actual filming. The camera operator may even have a support team of assistants. The *first assistant camera operator* will typically focus on the cameras, making sure they are loaded and operating correctly and conferring with lighting specialists. In larger productions, there are also backup cameras and accessories for use if one should malfunction during filming. *Second assistant camera operators* help the first assistant set up scenes to be filmed and assist in the maintenance of the equipment.

Sometimes camera operators must use shoulder-held cameras. This often occurs during the filming of action scenes for television or motion pictures. *Special effects camera operators* photograph the optical effects segments for motion pictures and television. They create visual illusions that can add mood and tone to the motion picture. They usually add fades, dissolves, superimpositions, and other effects to their films at the request of the *director of photography,* also known as the *director of cinematography* or the *cinematographer.*

## REQUIREMENTS

### High School
Take classes that will prepare you for the technical aspect of the work—courses in photography, journalism, and media arts should give you some hands-on experience with a camera. Mathematics and science can help you in understanding cameras and filters. You should also take art and art history classes and other courses that will help you develop appreciation of visual styles.

### Postsecondary Training
A college degree is not necessary to get a position as a motion picture camera operator, but attending film school can help you expand your network of connections. A bachelor's degree in liberal arts or film studies provides a good background for work in the film industry, but practical experience and industry connections will provide the best

opportunities for work. Upon completing an undergraduate program, you may wish to enroll in a master's program at a film school. Some schools offering well-established programs are the School of Visual Arts in New York, New York University, and the University of Southern California. These schools have film professionals on their faculties and provide a very visible stage for student talent, being located in the two film business hot spots—New York and California. Film school offers overall formal training, providing an education in fundamental skills by working with student productions. Such education is rigorous, but in addition to teaching skills it provides you with peer groups and a network of contacts with students, faculty, and guest speakers that can be of help after graduation.

### Other Requirements
You must be able to work closely with other members of a film crew and to carefully follow the instructions of the cinematographer and other camera operators. Since lighting is an integral part of filmmaking, you should have a thorough understanding of lighting equipment in order to work quickly and efficiently. In addition to the technical aspects of filmmaking, you should also understand the artistic nature of setting up shots.

## EXPLORING

To gain experience in this field, you should join a photography or camera club, or become involved with the media department of your school. You may have the opportunity then to shoot sports events, concerts, and school plays. You can also learn about photography by working in a camera shop. A part-time job in a camera shop will give you a basic understanding of photographic equipment. Some school districts have television stations where students can learn the basics of camera operation. This kind of hands-on experience is invaluable when looking for work in the field. You can also learn about the film industry by reading such publications as *American Cinematographer* (http://www.theasc.com/magazine), *ICG Magazine* (http://icg magazine.com), and *Cinefex* (http://www.cinefex.com).

## EMPLOYERS

There are approximately 27,000 television, video, and movie camera operators working in the United States. About 17 percent of these operators are self-employed. The majority of camera operators who are salaried employees work for the film and television industry at TV stations or film studios. Most jobs are found in large, urban areas.

## STARTING OUT

Most entry-level jobs require little formal preparation in photography or camera operation. A college degree is not required by most film or television studios, but you may have to belong to the International Cinematographers Guild, the national union for camera operators. An entry-level job as a camera assistant usually begins with assignments such as setting up or loading film into cameras and adjusting or checking lighting. With experience, the assistant may participate in decisions about what to photograph or how to film a particular scene.

Before you receive any paying jobs, you may have to volunteer or intern on a film project. You can surf the Internet for postings of openings on film productions, or contact your state's film commission.

## ADVANCEMENT

It usually takes two to four years for a motion picture camera operator to learn the techniques necessary for the job. Those who become proficient in their field, after several years of training, may be able to work on film projects as a cinematographer or director of photography (DP). The DP supervises other camera operators and works more closely with the directors, producers, and actors in the creation of the film. Some camera operators study cinematography part time while keeping their jobs as camera operators. They may later move to larger studios or command higher salaries.

## EARNINGS

Self-employed camera operators typically work on a project-by-project basis and may have periods of unemployment between jobs. Those working on movies may be paid per-day, and their role in the creation of the movie may last anywhere from several weeks to several months. Camera operators who are salaried employees of, for example, a television network have steady, year-round employment. Because of these factors and others, such as area of the country in which the operator works and the size of the employer, salaries vary widely for these professionals. The U.S. Department of Labor reports the median annual earnings of all television, video, and movie camera operators were $41,850 in 2007. The department also reports that the lowest paid 10 percent of operators earned less than $21,050 per year, but at the top end of the pay scale, the highest earning 10 percent made more than $78,330 annually.

A camera operator in Tanzania films women and children dancing. *(Sean Sprague, The Image Works)*

Salaried employees usually receive benefits such as health insurance, retirement plans, and vacation days. Those who are self-employed must pay for such extras themselves.

## WORK ENVIRONMENT

Motion picture camera operators work indoors and outdoors. Most work for motion picture studios or in television broadcasting. During filming, a camera operator may spend several weeks or months on location in another city or country. Most often the camera operator lives and works in their home city and works during regular business hours. Hours can be erratic, however, if the film includes scenes that must be shot at night, or if a deadline must be met by after-hours filming.

Much of the work of a camera operator becomes routine after a few years of experience. Camera operators get used to loading and unloading film, carrying cameras and equipment from trucks or workshops into studios or sets, and filming segments over and over again. The glamour of working on motion pictures or television programs may be diminished by the physically demanding work. Also, the actors, directors, and producers are the individuals in the limelight. They often receive credit for the work the camera operators have done.

Many camera operators must be available to work on short notice. Since motion picture camera operators are generally hired to work on one film at a time, there may be long periods during which a camera operator is not working. Few can make a living as self-employed camera operators.

Motion picture camera operators working on documentary or news productions may work in dangerous places. Sometimes they must work in uncomfortable positions or make adjustments for imperfect lighting conditions. They usually operate their cameras while standing for hours at a time. Deadline pressure is also a constant in the camera operator's work. Working for directors or producers who are on tight budgets or strict schedules may be very stressful.

## OUTLOOK

Employment for camera operators is expected to increase about as fast as the average for all occupations through 2016, according to the U.S. Department of Labor. The use of visual images continues to grow in areas such as communication, education, entertainment, marketing, and research and development. The growth of the Internet will generate many new opportunities for camera operators to create made-for-the-Internet broadcasts. More businesses will make use of training films and public relations projects that use film. The entertainment industries, especially motion picture production and distribution, are also expanding. However, competition for positions is very fierce. Camera operators work in what is considered a desirable and exciting field, and they must work hard and be aggressive to get good jobs, especially in Los Angeles and New York. They must also have strong computer skills in order to master rapidly changing technologies and filmmaking techniques.

## FOR MORE INFORMATION

*For lists of tricks of the trade and favorite films of famous cinematographers, visit the ASC Web site.*
**American Society of Cinematographers (ASC)**
PO Box 2230
Hollywood, CA 90078-2230
Tel: 800-448-0145
Email: info@theasc.com
http://www.theasc.com

*For information on membership benefits, contact this branch of the International Alliance of Theatrical Stage Employees (IATSE).*

**International Cinematographers Guild (IATSE Local 600)**
National Office/Western Region
7715 Sunset Boulevard
Hollywood, CA 90046-3911
Tel: 323-876-0160
http://www.cameraguild.com

*To learn about student chapters sponsored by the SMPTE, contact*
**Society of Motion Picture and Television Engineers (SMPTE)**
595 West Hartsdale Avenue
White Plains, NY 10601-1509
Tel: 914-761-1100
Email: smpte@smpte.org
http://www.smpte.org

# Cinematographers and Directors of Photography

## QUICK FACTS

**School Subjects**
Art
English

**Personal Skills**
Artistic
Technical/scientific

**Work Environment**
Indoors and outdoors
Primarily multiple locations

**Minimum Education Level**
Bachelor's degree

**Salary Range**
$21,050 to $41,850 to
$78,330+

**Certification or Licensing**
None available

**Outlook**
About as fast as the average

**DOT**
143

**GOE**
01.08.01

**NOC**
5131

**O*NET-SOC**
27-4031.00

## OVERVIEW

The *cinematographer,* also known as the *director of photography (DP),* is instrumental in establishing the mood of a film by putting the narrative aspects of a script into visual form. The cinematographer is responsible for every shot's framing, lighting, color level, and exposure—elements that set the artistic tone of a film.

## HISTORY

Motion picture cameras were invented in the late 1800s. In 1903, Edwin Porter made *The Great Train Robbery,* the first motion picture that used modern filmmaking techniques to tell a story. Porter filmed the scenes out of sequence and then edited and spliced them together to make the film, as is done today.

In the early years of film, the director handled the camera and made the artistic decisions that today are the job of the director of photography. The technical sophistication and artistic choices that are part of today's filming process had not yet emerged; instead, directors merely filmed narratives without moving the camera. Lighting was more for functional purposes of illumination than for artistic effect. Soon, however, directors began to experiment. They moved the camera to shoot from different angles and established a variety of editing techniques.

In the 1950s, the dominance of major studios in film production was curbed by an antitrust court decision, and more independent films were made. Changes in the U.S. tax code made independent producing more profitable. New genres and trends challenged the director and artistic staff of a production. Science fiction, adventure, mystery, and romance films grew in popularity. By the late 1960s, university film schools were established to train students in directing and cinematography as well as in other areas.

New developments in technologies and equipment have continued to influence both how films are made and how they look. The end of the 20th century and the beginning of the 21st saw the production of movies incorporating such elements as computer graphics, digital imaging, and digital color. Films such as *Titanic, Gladiator, Lord of the Rings,* and the latest episodes of *Star Wars* presented new visual challenges to filmmakers in terms of the amount and complexity of special effects needed in the films. DPs lead the way in understanding and using new technologies to push the art of filmmaking into a new, digital era.

## THE JOB

Cinematographers consider how the look of a film helps to tell its story. How can the look enhance the action, the emotions expressed, or the characters' personalities? Should the scene be filmed from across the room or up close to the actors? Should the lighting be stark or muted? How does the angle of the camera contribute to the scene? These are just some of the questions DPs must answer when composing a shot. Because DPs have both artistic and technical knowledge, they are integral members of the production team. They work in both film and television, helping directors to interpret a script and bring it to life.

At the beginning of a project, the DP reads the script and talks to the director about how to film each scene. Together they determine how to achieve the desired effects by deciding on camera angles and movement, lighting, framing, and which filters to use. By manipulating effects, DPs help determine the mood of a scene. For example, to raise the level of tension and discomfort in an argument, the DP can tell a camera operator to film at an unusual angle or move around the actors as they speak. The director may choose to film a scene in more than one way and then decide which best suits the project. With good collaboration between the director and the DP, decisions will be made quickly and successfully.

DPs are responsible for assembling the camera crew and telling crew members how to film each scene. They must be knowledgeable about all aspects of camera operation, lighting, filters, and types of film. There are multiple ways an effect can be approached, and DPs must be aware of them in order to make suggestions to the director and to capture the mood desired.

For small, low-budget films, some of the crew's roles may be combined. For example, the DP may operate a camera in addition to overseeing the crew. In a large production, the crew's roles will be more specialized. The *camera operator* either operates the camera physically or controls it remotely, using a control panel. The *first assistant camera operator* helps with focus, changes lenses and filters, sets the stop for film exposure, and makes sure the camera is working properly. Camera focus is extremely important and is not judged simply by how the shot looks to the eye. Instead, the first assistant carries a measuring tape and measures all the key positions of the actors and makes calculations to ensure correct focus. The *second assistant camera operator,* also called the *loader,* loads film magazines, keeps track of how much film stock is left, and keeps camera reports. Camera reports record which shots the director likes and wants to have printed. A *gaffer* leads the electrical crew, and the *grips* handle the dollies and cranes to move the cameras.

When shooting begins, cinematographers take a series of test shots of film locations to determine the lighting, lenses, and film stock that will work best. Once filming starts, they make adjustments as necessary. They may also film screen tests of actors so the director can be sure they are right for their parts.

Richard Shore, A.S.C., has had a career that extends over 40 years, 20 countries, and 200 films. His feature work includes *Bang the Drum Slowly,* a film that Robert DeNiro credits as starting his career. Currently, Shore is a lecturer at the New York Film Academy, where he teaches basic and advanced courses in filmmaking and works one-on-one with students. He teaches classes in cinematography, lighting, scripts, and other aspects of filmmaking.

One of Shore's early filmmaking jobs was making training films for the U.S. Army during the Korean War. "After the war," he says, "I got work making travel films, documentaries, industrial films. I also made TV commercials." This eventually led to a career filled with awards, including two Oscars, three Emmys, and induction into the American Society of Cinematographers.

Different projects have different demands; for one of the films for which he won an Oscar, a short film about poet Robert Frost, Shore was involved in many aspects of the filmmaking process beyond the duties of DP. For one of his Emmy-winning projects, Shore worked as a director. While working on a documentary about French president Francois Mitterand, Shore traveled extensively, spending two months with Mitterand in Paris, then flying with him to Washington D.C. to meet with President Reagan. "In the film industry," Shore says, "you have experiences you can't get anywhere else."

# REQUIREMENTS

## High School

To prepare for a career in cinematography, you should take college-preparatory courses such as math, English, government, and foreign language. Courses in English composition and literature will give you a background in narrative development, and art and photography courses can help you understand the basics of lighting and composition. A broadcast journalism or media course may give you some hands-on experience in camera operation and video production.

## Postsecondary Training

A bachelor's degree in liberal arts or film studies provides a good background for work in the film industry, but practical experience and industry connections will provide the best job opportunities. Upon completing an undergraduate program, you may wish to enroll in a master's program or master's of fine arts program at a film school. Schools offering well-established programs include the School of Visual Arts in New York, New York University, and the University of Southern California. These schools have film professionals on their faculties and provide a very visible stage for student talent. In addition to classroom time, film school offers students the opportunity to work on their own productions. Such education is rigorous, but in addition to teaching skills it encourages peer groups and creates a network of contacts among students, faculty, and guest speakers that can be useful after graduation.

An alternative to film school is the New York Film Academy (NYFA). NYFA gives students an idea of the demands of filmmaking careers by immersing them in short, but intensive, workshops. During this time, students have access to cameras and editing tables and are required to make short films of their own. (Contact information for all schools is listed at the end of this article.)

"A lot of people want to make films," Richard Shore says, "but there is really no direct route to entering the film industry. All production companies care about is what you can show them that you've done. You need to make a short film and submit it to a festival. If it's shown and gets recognition, that's your entrée."

## Other Requirements

You'll need to keep abreast of technological innovations while working in the industry. You must be comfortable with the technical as well as artistic aspects of the profession. You also must be a good leader to make decisions and direct your crew effectively.

"You really have to want it," Shore says about the work of a DP. "It's almost like a calling. You can't go into it half-way." Shore says it's also helpful to have your own original story ideas when embarking on a film career. "Film is a storytelling art, a narrative art. Someone with the ideal background is someone interested in literature, particularly the novel."

## EXPLORING

With cable television, videos, the Internet, and DVDs, it is much easier to study films today than it was 25 years ago. It's likely to become even easier as the Internet might someday enable you to download any film you choose. Take full advantage of the availability of great films and study them closely for different filmmaking styles. The documentary *Visions of Light: The Art of Cinematography,* directed by Arnold Glassman, Todd McCarthy, and Stuart Samuels, is a good introduction to some of the finest cinematography in the history of film. You can also experiment with composition and lighting if you have access to a 16-millimeter camera, a camcorder, or a digital camera. Check with your school's media center or journalism department about recording school events. Your school's drama club can also introduce you to the elements of comedy and drama and may involve you with writing and staging your own productions.

Subscribe to *American Cinematographer* magazine or read selected articles at the magazine's Web site (http://www.theasc.com/magazine). Other industry magazines such as *ICG Magazine* (http://icgmagazine. com), *Daily Variety* (http://www.variety.com), *Hollywood Reporter* (http://www.hollywoodreporter.com), and *Cinefex* (http://www.cine fex.com) can also give you insight into filmmaking.

## EMPLOYERS

Motion picture studios, production companies, independent producers, and documentary filmmakers all employ DPs, either as salaried employees or as freelancers. The U.S. Department of Labor reports that 17 percent of all camera operators work on a freelance basis. Most freelancers are responsible for finding their own projects to work on, but a few are represented by agents who solicit work for them.

## STARTING OUT

Internships are a very good way to gain experience and help you to become a marketable job candidate. Since local television stations and lower budget film productions operate with limited funds, they may offer internships for course credit or experience instead of a salary. You should check with your state's film commission to learn

Cinematographers must have good leadership skills in order to make decisions and direct their crew effectively. *(Topham/The Image Works)*

of productions in your area and volunteer to work in any capacity. Many production opportunities are also posted on the Web. By working on productions, you'll develop relationships with crew members and production assistants, and you'll be able to build a network of industry connections.

Before working as a DP, you'll likely work as a camera assistant or production assistant. To prepare yourself for this work, try to gain some experience in camera work with a college broadcasting station, a local TV crew, or advertising agency.

Cinematographers may choose to join a union because some film studios will hire only union members. The principal union for this field is the International Cinematographers Guild. Union members work under a union contract that determines their work rules, pay, and benefits.

## ADVANCEMENT

The position of cinematographer is in itself an advanced position. Richard Shore says securing a job as a DP "takes years and years of training. You must work your way up from first assistant, to camera operator, to DP. It's not a union thing, it's a way of learning. You learn from watching cinematographers work."

Those wanting to be DPs must get a foot in the door by making short films and getting them seen by producers. "Not only do you need skills, but you must make connections with people," Shore explains.

Camera operators may have opportunities to work as cinematographers on some projects. As they continue to develop relationships with filmmakers and producers, their DP work may increase, leading to better paying, high-profile film projects. Once a DP has begun working in the industry, advancement may come as the DP develops a reputation for excellent, innovative work. Directors and producers may then request to work with that particular DP, which can also lead to higher pay.

## EARNINGS

Many DPs do freelance work or have jobs under union contracts. They may work for a variety of employers ranging from major studios producing films with multimillion-dollar budgets to small,

## Award Winners

Want to see the best of the best? Here's a selection of films that have won an Oscar for cinematography:

1940: *Rebecca* (cinematography by George Barnes)

1952: *The Quiet Man* (Winton C. Hoch and Archie Stout)

1959: *The Diary of Anne Frank* (William C. Mellor)

1965: *Doctor Zhivago* (Freddie Young)

1969: *Butch Cassidy and the Sundance Kid* (Conrad Hall)

1977: *Close Encounters of the Third Kind* (Vilmos Zsigmond)

1979: *Apocalypse Now* (Vittorio Storaro)

1988: *Mississippi Burning* (Peter Biziou)

1993: *Schindler's List* (Janusz Kaminski)

1996: *The English Patient* (John Seale)

1997: *Titanic* (Russell Carpenter)

2001: *The Lord of the Rings: The Fellowship of the Ring* (Andrew Lesnie)

2005: *Memoirs of a Geisha* (Dion Beebe)

2007: *There Will Be Blood* (Robert Elswit)

Source: Academy of Motion Picture Arts and Sciences

independent producers who are financing a film with their credit cards. As a result, their earnings vary widely.

When starting out as a camera operator, an individual may volunteer for a job, without pay, simply to get experience. At the other end of the earnings scale, a well-established DP working on big-budget productions can make well over $1 million a year. IATSE establishes minimum wage scales for DPs who are union members, based on the nature of a film shoot. For feature film studio shoots, a cinematographer is paid about $520 a day. For location shoots, the wage is about $670 a day. Special provisions for holiday and overtime work are also made.

For an idea of what the average cinematographer may make in a year, consider government findings. The U.S. Department of Labor, which categorizes DPs with all camera operators, reports the median annual earnings for camera operators were $41,850 in 2007. The lowest paid 10 percent of camera operators, including those working in television and video, made less than $21,050. At the high end, 10 percent earned more than $78,330.

Freelancers must pay for their own benefits, such as health insurance, and they usually must buy their own equipment, which can be quite expensive.

## WORK ENVIRONMENT

Working conditions vary depending on the size and nature of the production. In television production and in movies, DPs may work both indoors and outdoors. Indoors, conditions can be cramped, while outdoors there may be heat, cold, rain, or snow. DPs may need to travel for weeks at a time while a project is being shot on location, and some locations, such as the middle of a desert, may mean staying miles from civilization. Hours can be long and the shooting schedule rigorous, especially when a film is going over budget. DPs work as members of a team, instructing assistants while also taking instruction from directors and producers. Those making a film with a small budget may be required to oversee many different aspects of the production.

Filming challenges, such as how to shoot effectively underwater, in the dark, or in public areas, are a normal part of the job. DPs need patience in setting up cameras and preparing the lighting, as well as in dealing with the variety of professionals with whom they work.

"If you can get into film," Richard Shore says, "it's a wonderful career." One reason DPs enjoy their work so much is that they work with talented, artistic, and skillful professionals. "There's a camaraderie among film crew members," Shore says.

## OUTLOOK

The U.S. Department of Labor predicts that employment for camera operators will grow about as fast as the average for all careers through 2016. More opportunities, though, will be available for those willing to work outside of the film industry at, for example, advertising agencies and TV broadcasting companies. The department anticipates that other types of programming, such as Internet broadcasts of music videos, sports, and other shows, will provide job openings in this field.

However, competition for work will be fierce because so many people are attracted to this business. "There are so many more qualified people than there are jobs," Richard Shore says. "It's impossible to guarantee success." Nevertheless, those with the right connections, strong samples of their work, and some luck are likely to find opportunities.

DPs of the future will be working more closely with special effects houses, even on films other than science fiction, horror, and other genres typically associated with special effects. Digital technology is used to create crowd scenes, underwater images, and other effects more efficiently and economically. DPs will have to approach a film with an understanding of which shots can be produced digitally and which will require traditional methods of filmmaking.

## FOR MORE INFORMATION

*For information about education and training workshops for television and film production and to read about events in the industry, visit the AFI Web site.*

**American Film Institute (AFI)**
2021 North Western Avenue
Los Angeles, CA 90027-1625
Tel: 323-856-7600
http://www.afi.com

*This Web site has information on the ASC, articles from* American Cinematographer *magazine, industry news, and a students' section with grants and fellowship information. The ASC online store sells many helpful publications covering aspects of film production.*

**American Society of Cinematographers (ASC)**
PO Box 2230
Hollywood, CA 90078-2230
Tel: 800-448-0145
Email: info@theasc.com
http://www.theasc.com

*For information on membership benefits, contact this branch of the International Alliance of Theatrical Stage Employees (IATSE).*

**International Cinematographers Guild (IATSE Local 600)**
National Office/Western Region
7715 Sunset Boulevard
Hollywood, CA 90046-3911
Tel: 323-876-0160
http://www.cameraguild.com

*To read about film programs at several schools, visit the following Web sites:*

**New York Film Academy**
http://www.nyfa.com

**New York University**
http://filmtv.tisch.nyu.edu/page/home

**School of Visual Arts**
http://schoolofvisualarts.edu

**University of Southern California**
http://cinema.usc.edu

# Conservators and Conservation Technicians

## QUICK FACTS

**School Subjects**
Art
Chemistry

**Personal Skills**
Mechanical/manipulative
Technical/scientific

**Work Environment**
Primarily indoors
Primarily one location

**Minimum Education Level**
Bachelor's degree

**Salary Range**
$20,000 to $35,350 to
$62,640+

**Certification or Licensing**
None available

**Outlook**
Faster than the average

**DOT**
102

**GOE**
01.06.01

**NOC**
5112, 5212

**O*NET-SOC**
25-4013.00

## OVERVIEW

*Conservators* analyze and assess the condition of artifacts and pieces of art, plan for the care of art collections, and carry out conservation treatments and programs. Conservators may be in private practice or work for museums, historical societies, or state institutions. When conserving artifacts or artwork, these professionals must select methods and materials that preserve and retain the original integrity of each piece. Conservators must be knowledgeable about the objects in their care, which may be natural objects, such as bones and fossils, or man-made objects, such as paintings, photographs, sculpture, paper, and metal.

*Conservation technicians* work under the supervision of conservators and complete maintenance work on the collection.

## HISTORY

Conservation is the youngest of all museum disciplines. The word *conservation* has been used in reference to works of art only since approximately 1930. For at least a century before 1930, museums may have employed *restorers,* or *restoration specialists,* but the philosophy that guided their work was much different than the ideas and values held by conservators today. Early conservators were often tradespeople, artists, or framers called upon to restore a damaged work of art to an approximate version of its original condition.

They repainted, varnished, or patched objects as they saw fit, working independently and experimenting as necessary to achieve the desired results. Conservators today use highly scientific methods and recognize the need both to care for works of art before deterioration occurs and to treat objects after damage has been done.

The first regional conservation laboratory in the United States, known as the Intermuseum Conservation Association, was created in 1952 in Oberlin, Ohio, when several smaller museums joined to bring their skills together.

Thanks to increasingly precise cleaning methods and scientific inventions such as thermal adhesives, the science of conservation has advanced. Today, the field is highly specialized and those who work in it must face demanding standards and challenges.

## THE JOB

Conservation professionals generally choose to specialize in one area of work that is defined by medium, such as in the preservation of photographic materials, books and paper, architecture, objects, paintings, textiles, or wooden artifacts. Common conservation issues associated with photographs, for example, include torn, bent, or cracked photos; deteriorated or soiled negatives; photographs or negatives that are adhered to enclosures; and damage to materials found in photographic media such as glass, plastic film, metal, and composite objects including paper, paper prints, wood, and album/book structures. There are also conservators who specialize in archaeology or ethnographic materials. Many are employed by museums, while others provide services through private practice. Conservation activities include carrying out technical and scientific studies on art objects, stabilizing the structure and reintegrating the appearance of cultural artifacts, and establishing the environment in which artifacts are best preserved. A conservator's responsibilities also may include documenting the structure and condition through written and visual recording, designing programs for preventive care, and executing conservation treatments. Conservation tools include microscopes and cameras and equipment for specialized processes such as infrared and ultraviolet photography and X rays.

Conservation technicians assist conservators in preserving or restoring artifacts and art objects. To do this, they study descriptions and information about the object and may perform chemical and physical tests and treatments as specified by the conservator. If a photograph is torn, for example, a technician may repair it using dry wheat starch paste and thin Japanese tissue. To remove adhesive residue or tape (which are harmful to photographs over time), a technician may clean the residue gently with a slightly damp swab or use a hot air pump and scalpel. Technicians may also make and repair picture frames and mount paintings in frames.

A *conservation scientist* is a professional scientist whose primary focus is in developing materials and knowledge to support conservation activities. Some specialize in scientific research into artists' materials, such as paints and varnishes or photographic emulsions. *Conservation educators* have substantial knowledge and experience in the theory and practice of conservation and have chosen to direct their efforts toward teaching the principles, methodology, and technical aspects of the profession. *Preparators* supervise the installation of specimens, art objects, and artifacts, often working with design technicians, curators, and directors to ensure the safety and preservation of items on display.

## REQUIREMENTS

### High School

Good conservation work comes from a well-balanced formulation of art and science. To prepare for a career in conservation, concentrate on doing well in all academic subjects, including courses in chemistry, natural science, history, and the arts.

### Postsecondary Training

In the past, many conservation professionals received their training solely through apprenticeships with experienced conservators. The same is not true today; you will need a bachelor's degree to find work as a technician, and in all but the smallest institutions you will need a master's degree to advance to conservator. Because graduate programs are highly selective, you should plan your academic path with care.

At the undergraduate level, take course work in the sciences, including inorganic and organic chemistry, the humanities (art history, archaeology, and anthropology), and studio art. Some graduate programs will consider work experience and gained expertise in conservation practice as comparable to coursework when screening applicants. In addition, most graduate programs recognize a student's participation in apprenticeship or internship positions while also completing coursework as an indication of the applicant's commitment to the career.

### Other Requirements

Conservation can be physically demanding. Conservators and conservation technicians must concentrate on specific physical and mental tasks for long periods of time. Endurance, manual dexterity, and patience are often needed to complete projects successfully.

# EXPLORING

If you are considering a career in the conservation of art (including photographs and motion pictures) or artifacts, try contacting local museums or art conservation laboratories that may allow tours or interviews. Read trade or technical journals (such as *Topics in Photographic Preservation*, which is published by the Photographic Materials Group) to gain a sense of the many issues that conservators address. Contact professional organizations, such as the American Institute for Conservation of Historic and Artistic Works, for directories of training and conservation programs.

Because employment in this field, even at entry level, most often entails handling precious materials and cultural resources, you should be fairly well prepared before contacting professionals to request either an internship or a volunteer position. You need to demonstrate a high level of academic achievement and have a serious interest in the career to edge out the competition for a limited number of jobs.

# EMPLOYERS

Museums, libraries, historical societies, private conservation laboratories, and government agencies hire conservators and conservation technicians. Institutions with small operating budgets sometimes hire part-time specialists to perform conservation work. This is especially common when curators need extra help in preparing items for display. Antique dealers may also seek the expertise of an experienced conservator for merchandise restoration, identification, and appraisal purposes.

# STARTING OUT

Most often students entering the field of art conservation have completed high school and undergraduate studies, and many are contemplating graduate programs. At this point a student is ready to seek a position (often unpaid) as an apprentice or intern with either a private conservation company or a museum to gain a practical feel for the work. Training opportunities are scarce and in high demand. Prospective students must convince potential trainers of their dedication to the highly demanding craft of conservation. The combination of academic or formal training along with hands-on experience and apprenticeship is the ideal foundation for entering the career.

# ADVANCEMENT

Due to rapid changes in each conservation specialty, practicing conservators must keep abreast of advances in technology and methodology. Conservators stay up to date by reading publications, attending professional meetings, and enrolling in short-term workshops or courses.

An experienced conservator wishing to move into another realm of the field may become a private consultant, an appraiser of art or artifacts, a conservation educator, a curator, or a museum registrar.

## EARNINGS

Salaries for conservators vary greatly depending on the level of experience, chosen specialty, region, job description, and employer. The U.S. Department of Labor, which classifies conservators with curators, museum technicians, and archivists, reports the median annual earnings for this group as $35,350 in 2007. The lowest paid 10 percent of this group earned less than $21,630, and the highest paid 10 percent made more than $62,640.

According to the American Institute for Conservation of Historic and Artistic Works, a first year conservator can expect to earn approximately $20,000 annually. Conservators with several years of experience report annual earnings between $35,000 and $40,000. Senior conservators have reported earnings between $50,000 and $60,000 annually.

Fringe benefits, including paid vacations, medical and dental insurance, sick leave, and retirement plans, vary according to each employer's policies.

## WORK ENVIRONMENT

Conservation work may be conducted indoors, in laboratories, or in an outdoor setting. Conservators typically work 40 to 60 hours per week depending on exhibit schedules and deadlines, as well as the amount and condition of unstable objects in their collections. Because some conservation tasks and techniques involve the use of toxic chemicals, laboratories are equipped with ventilation systems. At times a conservator may find it necessary to wear a mask and possibly even a respirator when working with particularly harsh chemicals or varnishes. Most of the work requires meticulous attention to detail, a great deal of precision, and manual dexterity.

The rewards of the conservation profession are the satisfaction of preserving artifacts that reflect the diversity of human achievements; being in regular contact with art, artifacts, and structures; enjoying a stimulating workplace; and the creative application of expertise to the preservation of artistically and historically significant objects.

# OUTLOOK

The U.S. Department of Labor predicts the employment of museum conservators and technicians will grow faster than the average for all careers through 2016. Competition for these desirable positions, however, will be strong.

The public's developing interest in cultural material of all forms will contribute to the growth of art conservation and preservation. New specialties have emerged in response to the interest in collections maintenance and preventive care. Conservation, curatorial, and registration responsibilities are intermingling and creating hybrid conservation professional titles, such as collections care, environmental monitoring, and exhibits specialists.

Despite these developments, however, any decreases in federal funding often affect employment and educational opportunities. For example, in any given year, if Congress limits government assistance to the National Endowment for the Arts, less money is available to assist students through unpaid internships. As museums experience a tightening of federal funds, many may choose to decrease the number of paid conservators on staff and instead rely on a small staff augmented by private conservation companies that can be contracted on a short-term basis as necessary. Private industry and for-profit companies will then continue to grow, while federally funded nonprofit museums may experience a reduction of staff.

# FOR MORE INFORMATION

*To receive additional information on conservation training, contact*
**American Institute for Conservation of Historic and
   Artistic Works**
Photographic Materials Group
1156 15th Street, NW, Suite 320
Washington, DC 20005-1714
Tel: 202-452-9545
Email: info@aic-faic.org
http://aic.stanford.edu
http://aic.stanford.edu/sg/pmg

*For more information on image presentation, contact*
**Image Permanence Institute**
Rochester Institute of Technology
70 Lomb Memorial Drive
Rochester, NY 14623-5604
Tel: 585-475-5199
http://www.imagepermanenceinstitute.org

*For information on internships and other learning opportunities in Canada, contact*
**Canadian Conservation Institute**
1030 Innes Road
Ottawa, ON K1A 0M5 Canada
Tel: 613-998-3721
http://www.cci-icc.gc.ca

―――――――――――― **INTERVIEW** ――――――――――――

*Katharine Whitman is a photo conservator in Toronto, Canada. (Visit http://www.photographconservation.com to learn more about her career.) She discussed her career with the editors of* Careers in Focus: Photography.

**Q. Where do you work?**

**A.** In September 2008 I started a contract as assistant photograph conservator at the Art Gallery of Ontario (the AGO), in Toronto, Canada. This is my first contract in the field. My position became permanent in April of 2009. Previously, I had a two-year fellowship at the George Eastman House International Museum of Photography and Film in Rochester, New York, after earning a master's of art conservation at Queen's University in Kingston, Ontario.

**Q. Can you please tell us a little about yourself and your work as a photo conservator?**

**A.** I am responsible for the well-being of all of the photographs in the collection at the AGO—more than 50,000 works. That number increases on a regular basis: the AGO is a collecting institution. My work consists of assessing the stability of photographs in the collection and for exhibition, treating photographs when necessary, making recommendations to collections managers on how to properly store works, and collaborating with curators to create exhibits that respect the needs of the works. In addition to my work at the AGO, I have a personal research interest in glass-supported photographs and have published papers on their proper housing and stabilization.

**Q. How did you get your first job in the field?**

**A.** Networking. While I was in graduate school I started attending professional conferences related to my field. It is extremely important to go to these conferences not only to attend lectures on new advances in the field, but to learn networking skills. During school, I met Rosaleen Hill, a paper conservator in private practice in British Columbia, Canada. We stayed in touch and reconnected at a subsequent conference. Her friend, Joan Weir, the paper conservator at the Art Gallery of Ontario, mentioned to Rosaleen the gallery's need for a photographs conservator. Rosaleen knew that my fellowship at the Eastman House was ending soon and introduced me to Joan. After the conference I applied for the position. Having met Joan made my application much more attractive to the gallery because there was a face and personality "attached" to the application.

**Q. What is one thing that young people may not know about a career in photo conservation?**

**A.** A background in science, as well as art history, is required to become an art conservator—a combination many people find strange. All graduate programs in conservation require a background in chemistry, archaeology, art history, and, in some cases, foreign languages. I have undergraduate degrees in photography and fisheries and wildlife—both of which have been essential in my field. The practice of art conservation is a science. I use my knowledge in art history to identify the probable creation date of photographs, as well as my chemistry background to describe why they are deteriorating, or not, every day.

**Q. What are the most important personal and professional qualities for photo conservators?**

**A.** Knowledge of a wide range of materials is essential in the field of photograph conservation. The substrate of photographs can be on a wide range of materials, including paper, plastic, metal, fabric, glass, and leather. In addition, many different materials can be used to bind the image to the substrate. A photograph conservator needs to understand how all of these materials work together and react to the environment around them.

Because many photographs are extremely fragile, controlled motor skills and an organized treatment plan will make the difference between a treatment that is successful and one that is not.

To be successful in this field, it is also important to collaborate with your colleagues. Photograph conservation is a very small field. It is essential to stay connected to the professional community to keep informed on the latest innovations and to share your own research and observations.

**Q. What advice would you give to young people who are interested in the field?**

**A.** Go to museums and look at photographs of all kinds in the real world as much as possible. Merely looking at reprinted photographs in books will not teach you how to truly look at photographs. You need to be able to see the tonality of the image, the texture of the surface of the print, and all of the other subtle nuances that make a photograph a unique object. These qualities cannot be reproduced in books. The only way to become a good photograph conservator is to know what a photograph is really supposed to look like. Additionally, the only way to learn how to identify different photographic processes is to look at as many photographs as you can, under the guidance of someone already familiar with the various processes. Hopefully you will be able to find someone who has a good knowledge of these materials to teach you what to look for as you get started.

**Q. What is the future employment outlook for photo conservators?**

**A.** As with each innovation in photography, the past few years have seen the decline of film and paper production by manufacturers. Within the next 10 years, they will likely cease production altogether as digital photography takes over. While a photograph can be scanned into a computer and digitized, it is not possible to faithfully reproduce the detail of an original photograph inexpensively. Original photographs that have been produced in a chemically based process will become unique and more valued; therefore the field of photograph conservation is going to need more professionals.

# Exhibit Designers

## OVERVIEW

*Exhibit designers* plan, develop, and produce physical displays for exhibitions at museums and similar institutions. Designers work closely with museum directors, educators, curators, and conservators to create educational exhibits that focus on portions of the museum's collection while maintaining safe environmental conditions for the objects on display. Exhibit designers prepare both temporary and permanent exhibitions for a broad range of museum audiences. There are approximately 12,000 set and exhibit designers working in the United States.

## HISTORY

The very first museum prototypes housed books and documents. Museums evolved from these ancient libraries to storage areas for private collections. Eventually, ambitious private collectors began to organize the objects in their collections, first by type (for instance, placing all baskets together), and then by the objects' uniqueness. Private collections became notable if they contained objects that no other collection contained. Displays of this kind have always satisfied natural human curiosity.

Charles Willson Peale was responsible for opening the first natural history museum intended for public use. As Peale performed all the duties necessary to run his home-based museum, he may also be credited with developing the first exhibit designs in the United States. He exhibited his specimens in natural settings (comparable to modern-day dioramas) to present visitors with contextual information about his collections. As curious visitors began to explore his museum, he realized the need to protect his specimens from environmental damage. He placed the more valuable items in cabinets to protect them from careless hands and reduce the effects of everyday wear and tear. Peale's home museum grew to become the Philadelphia Museum, and with its development came techniques and theories about exhibiting art and cultural artifacts that remain useful today.

Although photography became popular soon after its invention, it was not viewed as an art form until much later, after a succession of great photographers had demonstrated the photographic medium to be flexible, immediate, and expressive. By the early 20th century, photographs were being displayed with other artwork in galleries and museums. In 1949, the George Eastman House International Museum of Photography & Film became the world's first museum dedicated to photography. It currently houses more than 400,000 photographs and negatives; 23,000 films and more than five million film stills; 43,000 publications; and more than 25,000 pieces of technology.

Today, there are many well-known museums of photography and art museums that have comprehensive photography sections—they provide a variety of rewarding career opportunities for exhibit designers.

## THE JOB

Exhibit designers play a key role in helping museums and similar institutions achieve their educational goals. Museums provide public access to and information about their collections to visitors and scholars. They accomplish this by designing exhibits that display objects and contain contextual information. Because museum visits are interactive experiences, exhibit designers have a responsibility to provide the visiting public with provocative exhibitions that contain visual, emotional, and intellectual components. To achieve this transfer of information, designers must create a nonverbal conversation between exhibits and observers.

The decision to construct a new exhibit is made in collaboration with museum curators, educators, conservators, exhibit designers, and the museum director. After a budget has been set, exhibit designers must meet regularly with curators, educators, and conservators throughout the planning stages. The purpose of each exhibit production is educational, and the team plans each exhibition so that it tells a story. A successful exhibit brings meaning to the objects on display through the use of informative labels (for example, providing a concise overview of early cameras), the logical placement of objects, and the construction of display areas that help to place the objects in proper context.

Planning, designing, and producing a new exhibit is a costly as well as a mentally and emotionally challenging project. Exhibit designers must work creatively during the planning and design stages while remaining flexible in their ideas for the exhibition. On many occasions, designers must compromise artistic integrity for the sake of object safety and educational quality. During exhibit installation, designers work closely with the production team, which consists of other designers, technicians, electricians, and carpenters. Lead designers oversee the exhibit installation and attend to last-minute preparations. Most permanent exhibits are planned four years in advance, while most temporary exhibits are allowed between six to 18 months for production.

Exhibit designers have additional responsibilities that include researching exhibit topics and new exhibit theories. Designers must also attend conventions of professional associations and contribute to the advancement of their field by writing scholarly articles about new display techniques.

## REQUIREMENTS

### High School

Exhibit designers, like the majority of museum professionals, need diverse educational backgrounds to perform well in their jobs. Designers must develop their creative and artistic skills and master mathematics courses. At the high school level, take courses in English, history, science, art, and foreign language. These courses will give you general background knowledge you can use to define educational components of exhibitions. Geometry, algebra, advanced

An exhibit designer prepares photographs for an exhibition. *(David Lassman, The Image Works/Syracuse Newspapers)*

math, and physics are essential courses for future designers. Exhibit plans must be drawn to scale (often using the metric system) and measurements must be precise. Computer skills are equally necessary as many designers use computer-aided drafting when planning exhibits. Finally, courses in studio art and drawing will introduce you to the hands-on nature of exhibit work.

### Postsecondary Training
Some postsecondary training, including college-level math, art, and design courses, is necessary, and most museums expect candidates for the position of exhibit designer to hold a bachelor's degree. Designers that specialize in a design-related subject and continue their studies in a museum's specialty, such as art, photography, history, or science, have an advantage in being hired by that type of museum.

Those who desire a director position in a museum's design department should consider acquiring an advanced degree.

### Other Requirements
Excellent communication skills are essential in this career. Exhibit designers must be able to clearly express their ideas to both museum staff members who collaborate on exhibit projects and to visitors through the display medium. Designing exhibits is mentally challenging and can be physically demanding. Exhibit designers should be artistic, creative, and knowledgeable about preparing safe display environments that accommodate valuable and fragile objects.

## EXPLORING
The best way to learn more about exhibit design is to consult with a professional in the field. Contact your local museum, historical society, or related institution to interview and possibly observe a designer at work. Remain informed of the many new challenges and theories that influence an exhibit designer's work. Joining a professional association, reading industry publications such as the American Association of Museums' *Museum* and *Aviso*, or volunteering in a museum or art gallery are all excellent ways to explore this career.

Experience with design in other settings can also contribute to developing the skills an exhibit designer needs. You should consider taking studio classes from a local art guild, offer to design school bulletin boards, or design stage sets for the school drama club or local theater company.

# Photography Museums on the Web

California Museum of Photography (Riverside, Calif.)
http://www.cmp.ucr.edu

Canadian Museum of Contemporary Photography
(Ottawa, ON)
http://cmcp.gallery.ca

Florida Museum of Photographic Arts (Tampa, Fla.)
http://www.fmopa.org

George Eastman House International Museum of
Photography & Film (Rochester, N.Y.)
http://www.eastmanhouse.org

Griffin Museum of Photography (Winchester, Mass.)
http://www.griffinmuseum.org

International Center of Photography (New York, N.Y.)
http://www.icp.org

The Museum of Contemporary Photography (Chicago, Ill.)
http://www.mocp.org

Museum of Photographic Arts (San Diego, Calif.)
http://www.mopa.org

Southeast Museum of Photography (Daytona Beach, Fla.)
http://www.smponline.org

## EMPLOYERS

Approximately 12,000 set and exhibit designers are employed in the United States. Museums and private companies that display collections hire exhibit designers. Historical societies, state and federal agencies with archives, and libraries also employ exhibit designers because of their specialized skills in developing thoughtful displays while considering object safety. Exhibit designers may also find work with private design firms as well as exhibition companies that create and distribute both temporary and permanent exhibits throughout the world.

## STARTING OUT

Students who wish to become exhibit designers should supplement their design courses with an internship in a museum or a related institution. Some museums offer full- or part-time positions to qualified candidates when they complete their internship hours. Publications such as *Aviso,* which is published monthly, contain classified advertisements for available museum positions. Contacting other professional associations for job listings is also an acceptable method of starting out. Museum positions are highly competitive, and having a proven history of experience is invaluable. Keep a portfolio of your design examples to show to potential employers.

## ADVANCEMENT

Experienced exhibit designers with appropriate academic credentials and a history of creating educational and visitor-friendly displays are well situated to move into supervisory positions with greater responsibility and design freedom. Exhibit designers may choose to acquire advanced degrees in specialties such as architecture or graphic design in order to achieve the director of exhibitions position. Appropriately educated exhibit designers wishing to move into another area of the museum field may learn to assist conservators, become museum educators, collections managers, curators, or registrars. Exhibit designers who leave museum work are well positioned to seek employment in private design firms.

## EARNINGS

Salaries for exhibit designers vary widely depending on the size, type, and location of the institution, as well as the education, expertise, and achievements of the designer. A 2003 salary survey conducted by the Association of Art Museum Directors reported that the average salary of a chief exhibit preparator is roughly $36,000. Earnings ranged from as low as $18,267 to as high as $121,000. The same survey reported that the median salary of an exhibit designer was approximately $50,000, but ranged from as low as $31,000 to as high as $175,000. Some larger or better funded museums, historical societies, and related institutions pay significantly more, while others may hire on a contractual basis for a predetermined design and installation fee.

The U.S. Department of Labor reports that median annual earnings for set and exhibit designers were $43,220 in 2007. Salaries ranged from less than $23,600 to more than $78,220.

Fringe benefits, including medical and dental insurance, paid vacations and sick leave, and retirement plans, vary according to each employer's policies.

## WORK ENVIRONMENT

Exhibit designers typically work 40 hours per week. Continual challenges and strict deadlines make an exhibit designer's work both creative and demanding. Flexibility in working hours may be a requirement of employment as exhibition installment frequently occurs after museum hours when visitors are not present.

Exhibit designers usually have an office or studio in a private area of the museum but often must work on the exhibit floors during design planning, installation, and tear-down periods. Designers must collaborate with curators, museum educators, and conservators throughout the exhibit planning stages to ensure the educational integrity of the exhibition as well as the safety of the objects.

The rewards for designing in a museum environment include a stimulating workplace where the design medium changes continually, the creative application of design expertise, and the satisfaction of educating visitors through the display of artistically and historically significant objects.

## OUTLOOK

The *Occupational Outlook Handbook* reports that employment for set and exhibit designers will grow faster than the average for all occupations through 2016. However, there is strong competition for museum jobs, so designers with experience will have an advantage when applying for positions. As museums continue to face tight budgets, museum directors may choose to contract with independent exhibition and design companies to install new exhibits instead of retaining a staff of in-house designers. Private industry and for-profit companies have continued to grow while nonprofit museums and similar institutions may be experiencing a reduction of staff or limited hiring of new employees.

## FOR MORE INFORMATION

*For information on museum careers, education, and internships, contact*
**American Association of Museums**
1575 Eye Street, NW, Suite 400
Washington, DC 20005-1113

Tel: 202-289-1818
http://www.aam-us.org

*For publications and recent news about art museums, contact*
**Association of Art Museum Directors**
120 East 56th Street, Suite 520
New York, NY 10022-3673
Tel: 212-754-8084
http://www.aamd.org

*For information on workshops, earnings, employment, and its quarterly journal, contact*
**New England Museum Association**
22 Mill Street, Suite 409
Arlington, MA 02476-4744
Tel: 781-641-0013
http://www.nemanet.org

# Fashion Photographers

## OVERVIEW

*Fashion photographers* work in the fashion industry and focus their skills specifically on styles of clothing and personal image. They take and develop pictures of people, places, and objects while using a variety of cameras and photographic equipment. The photographs are used to advertise new fashions, promote models, and popularize certain designers in both print and electronic formats. Approximately 122,000 photographers are employed in the United States; only a small percentage of these professionals specialize in fashion photography.

## HISTORY

The art of photography goes back only about 150 years. The discoveries that eventually led to photography began early in the 18th century when a German scientist, Dr. Johann H. Schultze, experimented with the action of light on certain chemicals. He found that when these chemicals were covered by dark paper they did not change color, but when they were exposed to sunlight, they darkened. In 1839, a French painter named Louis Daguerre became the first photographer when he invented the daguerreotype. These early images were developed onto small metal plates and could not be reproduced in multiple prints.

Although the daguerreotype was the sensation of its day, photography did not come into widespread use until the late 1800s, when George Eastman invented a simple camera and flexible roll film. With exposure to the negative, light-sensitive paper was used to make positive multiple copies of the image.

Advances in photographic technology allow today's fashion photographers to use several different cameras, change lenses, and use special filters all in one photo shoot. Technology also allows them to "touch up" the photographs during the developing process, removing any unwanted blemish or object from the picture.

## THE JOB

Fashion photographers create the pictures that sell clothing, cosmetics, shoes, accessories, and beauty products. They provide artwork to accompany editorial pieces in magazines such as *Glamour, Harper's Bazaar,* and *Vogue* and newspapers such as *Women's Wear Daily.* Although fashion photographers can work in any of several different areas of the fashion field, the advertising industry is probably their largest employer. Catalog companies employ photographers to provide images that will sell their merchandise through print or online publications.

Fashion photography is a specialized form of photography that requires working on a team with designers, editors, illustrators, models, hair stylists, photo stylists, and makeup artists. Shooting takes place in a studio or on location, indoors and outdoors. Photographers use cameras, film, filters, lenses, lighting equipment, props, and sets. Their first priority is to satisfy the client's requirements. Some photographers develop a unique artistic style that earns them recognition and higher earnings.

Fashion photographers must be artistically talented (able to visualize designs, use colors, and create style) and be adept at using technologies such as digital cameras and various computer programs designed to manipulate photographs.

Photographers may work as freelancers, handling all the business aspects that go along with being self-employed. Such responsibilities include keeping track of expenses, billing clients promptly and appropriately, and keeping their businesses going by lining up new jobs for when a current project ends.

Because the fashion world is extremely competitive and fast paced, fashion photographers tend to work long hours under the pressure of deadlines and demanding personalities.

## REQUIREMENTS

### High School

Creativity is probably the most important skill you must have for this field. There are a number of classes you can take in high school to help you determine the extent of your talent and prepare for this work. Naturally, take as many studio art classes as you can. Drawing, painting, and photography classes are especially helpful. Also, take computer classes that teach you about photo manipulation software and digital photography. Business, accounting, or mathematics classes will give you skills you will need to keep track of your accounts and run your own business. Take English or communication classes to develop your communication skills. You will be working with a variety of people, often as a member of a team, and you must be able to convey your ideas clearly and accurately follow directions.

**Postsecondary Training**

Although this is a career field in which you don't need to take a specific postsecondary educational route, there are a number of training options available. There are, for example, academic programs in fashion photography at many colleges, universities, and adult education centers. Some community and junior colleges offer associate's degrees in photography or commercial art. Photography studies will include shooting and processing techniques using both black-and-white and color film, digital technology, lighting, and composition. An advantage to pursuing education beyond high school is that it gives you an opportunity to build your portfolio. A portfolio is a collection of an artist's best work that shows prospective clients a variety of skills.

In addition to studying art and photography, it is advantageous to study clothing construction, fabrics, fashion design, and cosmetology.

**Certification or Licensing**

The Professional Photographic Certification Commission, which is affiliated with Professional Photographers of America, offers certification to general photographers. Visit http://certifiedphotographer. com for more information. Although certification is not required to work as a fashion photographer, having it could give you an advantage when looking for jobs.

**Other Requirements**

Photographers need excellent manual dexterity, good eyesight and color vision, and artistic ability. They need an eye for composition as well as the ability to work creatively with their chosen medium. Because they work with groups of people, they will need to be patient, accommodating, and professional. An eye for detail is essential. And, naturally, they should be interested in fashion and expressing style through images.

# EXPLORING

You can explore this field by taking photography classes both at school and through local organizations such as community centers. Also, consider joining a school photography or art club. These clubs will give you the opportunity to meet with others who share your interests and attend talks or meetings with professionals. Join the staff of the school yearbook, newspaper, or literary magazine. These publications often make use of visual art to accompany their text. Look for part-time or summer work at a camera store. This work experience will give you the opportunity to become familiar with many "tools of the trade." Explore your interest in the fashion field by reading fashion magazines that will keep you up to date on fashion trends, models, and photographers' and illustrators' work. Try drawing or sewing your own fashion creations. If you can't find work at a camera store, try getting a job at a clothing store. This will give you experience working with people and clothes, and you might even be able to offer fashion advice to customers.

# EMPLOYERS

More than 50 percent of all professional photographers and visual artists are self-employed. Others work for large retailers, magazines, newspapers, design or advertising firms, and fashion firms.

# STARTING OUT

If you have received a postsecondary degree, one of the best ways to start out in this business is to find a job through your school's career services office or by networking with alumni. Those who are interested in photography sometimes gain entry by working as assistants or trainees to established photographers. You may be asked to do such things as move lights, work in the darkroom, and schedule appointments, but you will also gain experience and make contacts in the field. Those who are financially able may go into business for themselves right away. However, it may take considerable time to establish yourself in the field and have a business that is profitable.

# ADVANCEMENT

Advancement for fashion photographers generally comes as they gain professional recognition. Freelance photographers who become known for the creativity and high quality of their work will have a growing client base. More clients translate into more jobs; more

Fashion photographers take pictures of a model as she walks the runway at a fashion show. *(Kokyat Choong, The Image Works)*

jobs translate into higher earnings. In addition, as photographers become better known, they can charge more for their services and be more selective about what jobs they take. Salaried photographers may either move up within their organization, taking on supervisory roles or working with specific accounts for example, or they may choose to start their own photography business.

## EARNINGS

According to the U.S. Department of Labor, the median annual earnings for salaried photographers was approximately $27,720 in 2007. The lowest paid 10 percent made less than $16,170, while the highest paid 10 percent made more than $59,890 per year. Mean annual earnings for photographers who worked for newspaper, periodical, book, and directory publishers were $40,070 in 2007.

Photographers running their own businesses and working on a freelance basis are typically paid by the job. The pay for these jobs may be based on such factors as the photographer's reputation, the prestige of the client (for example, a fashion magazine with an international readership will pay more than a local newspaper doing a Sunday fashion spread), and the difficulty of the work. For some of this work, photographers may make $250 per job. They may also get credit lines and receive travel expenses. As they gain experience, build a strong portfolio of published work, and acquire prestigious clients, photographers can make $2,000 per job or more. Freelance photographers who have national or international reputations may make in the hundreds of thousands of dollars or more per year. Freelance workers, unlike salaried artists, however, do not receive benefits such as health insurance and paid vacation or sick days.

## WORK ENVIRONMENT

Photographers' working conditions vary based on the job and the employer. They may need to put in long or irregular hours to meet print deadlines. For some jobs they will work in a comfortable studio, while for others they may be on location, working on a dark street, or in the snow, or at a crowded fashion show. Freelance photographers have the added pressure of continually seeking new clients and uncertain incomes. Establishing oneself in the field can take years, and this is also a stressful process. On the positive side, fashion photographers are able to enjoy working in creative environments where visual images are highly valued.

## OUTLOOK

According to the U.S. Department of Labor, employment for visual artists and photographers is expected to grow as fast as the average for all careers through 2016. For photographers specifically working in fashion, employment will likely be dependent on the prosperity of agencies involved with the fashion field, such as magazines, newspapers, advertising firms, and fashion houses. The outlook for these agencies currently looks strong. The popularity of American fashions around the world should create a demand for photographers who can effectively capture the latest styles. In addition, numerous outlets for fashion, such as online magazines and retail Web sites, will create a need for photographers.

Competition for jobs, however, will be keen since these positions are highly attractive to people with artistic ability and technical skill. In addition, the *Occupational Outlook Handbook* notes that the growing popularity of digital cameras and computer art programs can allow consumers and businesses to produce and access photographic images on their own. Despite this improved technology, the specialized skills of the trained photographer should still be in demand in the fashion world. Individuals who are creative and persistent in finding job leads and who are able to adapt to rapidly changing technologies will be the most successful.

# FOR MORE INFORMATION

*This organization is committed to improving conditions for all creators of graphic art and to raising standards for the entire industry.*
**Graphic Artists Guild**
32 Broadway, Suite 1114
New York, NY 10004-1612
Tel: 212-791-3400
http://www.gag.org

*This college offers programs in fashion design and advertising and design.*
**International Academy of Design and Technology at Chicago**
1 North State Street, Suite 500
Chicago, IL 60602-3302
Tel: 877-ACADEMY
http://www.iadtchicago.com

*This college offers programs in various art and design fields.*
**Savannah College of Art and Design**
Admission Department
PO Box 77300
Atlanta, GA 30357-1300
Tel: 404-253-2700
http://www.scad.edu

*This Web site allows you to browse through galleries of hundreds of established fashion photographers.*
**FashionBook.com**
http://www.fashionbook.com/photographers

*Visit this site for more career advice.*
**Fashion Net: How to Become a Fashion Photographer**
http://www.fashion.net/howto/photography

# Film and Television Editors

## OVERVIEW

*Film and television editors* perform an essential role in the motion picture and television industries. They take an unedited draft of film, videotape, or digital video and use specialized equipment to improve the draft until it is ready for viewing. It is the responsibility of the film or television editor to create the most effective product possible. There are approximately 21,000 film and television editors employed in the United States.

## HISTORY

The motion picture and television industries have experienced substantial growth in the United States. One effect of this growth is a steady demand for the essential skills that film and television editors provide. With recent innovations in computer technology, much of the work that these editors perform is accomplished using sophisticated computer programs. All of these factors have enabled many film and television editors to find steady work as salaried employees of film and television production companies and as independent contractors who provide their services on a per-job basis.

In the early days of the industry, editing was the responsibility of directors, studio technicians, or other film staffers. Now every film, videotape, and digital video including the most brief television advertisement, has an editor who is responsible for the continuity and clarity of the project.

# THE JOB

Film and television editors work closely with producers and directors throughout an entire project. These editors assist in the earliest phase, called preproduction, and during the production phase, when actual filming occurs. However, their skills are in the greatest demand during postproduction, when primary filming is completed.

During preproduction, in meetings with producers, editors learn about the objectives of the film or video. If the project is a television commercial, for example, the editor must be familiar with the product the commercial will attempt to sell. If the project is a feature-length motion picture, the editor must understand the story line. The producer may explain the larger scope of the project so that the editor knows the best way to approach the work when it is time to edit the film. In consultation with the director, editors may discuss the best way to accurately present the screenplay or script. They may discuss different settings, scenes, or camera angles even before filming or taping begins. With this kind of preparation, film and television editors are ready to practice their craft as soon as the production phase is complete.

When working on a feature film, editors may spend months on one project, while others may work on several shorter projects simultaneously.

Steve Swersky owns his own editorial company in Los Angeles, California, and he has done editing for commercials, films, and television. In his 20 years on the job, he has edited Jeep commercials and worked on coming-attractions trailers for such movies as *Titanic, Fargo,* and *The Usual Suspects.* Swersky's work involves taking the film that has been developed in labs and transferring it to videotape for him to watch. He uses nonlinear computer editing for his projects, as opposed to traditional linear systems involving many video players and screens. "The difference between linear and nonlinear editing," he says, "is like the difference between typing and using a word processing program. When you want to change a typewritten page, you have to retype it; with word processing you can just cut and paste." Swersky uses the Lightworks nonlinear editing system. With this system, he converts the film footage to a digital format. The computer has a database that tracks individual frames and puts all the scenes together in a folder of information. This information is stored on a hard drive and can instantly be brought up on a screen, allowing an editor to access scenes and frames with the click of a mouse.

Editors are usually the final decision makers when it comes to choosing which segments will stay in as they are, which segments will be cut, or which may need to be redone. Editors look at the quality of the segment, its dramatic value, and its relationship to other segments. They then arrange the segments in an order that creates the most effective finished product. "I assemble the scenes," Swersky says, "choosing what is the best, what conveys the most emotion. I bring the film to life, in a way." He relies on the script and notes from the director, along with his natural sense of how a scene should progress, in putting together the film, commercial, or show. He looks for the best shots, camera angles, line deliveries, and continuity.

Some editors specialize in certain areas of television or film. *Sound editors* work on the soundtracks of television programs or motion pictures. They often keep libraries of sounds that they reuse for various projects. These include natural sounds, such as thunder or raindrops, animal noises, motor sounds, or musical interludes. Some sound editors specialize in music and may have training in music theory or performance. Others work with sound effects. They may use unusual objects, machines, or computer-generated noisemakers to create a desired sound for a film or TV show.

## REQUIREMENTS

### High School

Broadcast journalism and other media and communications courses may provide you with practical experience in video editing. Because film and television editing requires a creative perspective along with technical skills, you should take English, speech, theater, and other courses that will allow you to develop writing skills. Art and photography classes will involve you with visual media. If your high school offers classes in either film history or film production, be sure to take those courses. The American Film Institute hosts an educational Web site (http://www.afi.edu) that offers listings of high schools with film courses and other resources for teachers and students. Finally, don't forget to take computer classes. Editing work constantly makes use of new technology, and you should become familiar and comfortable with computers as soon as possible.

### Postsecondary Training

Some studios require a bachelor's degree for those seeking positions as film or television editors. However, actual on-the-job experience is the best guarantee of securing lasting employment. Degrees in liberal arts fields are preferred, but courses in cinematography and audiovisual techniques help editors get started in their work. You may choose to pursue a degree in such subjects as English, journalism, theater, or film. Community and two-year colleges often offer courses in the study of film as literature. Some of these colleges also teach film and video editing. Universities with departments of broadcast journalism offer courses in film and video editing and also may have contacts at local television stations.

Training as a film or television editor takes from four to 10 years. Many editors learn much of their work on the job as an assistant or apprentice at larger studios that offer these positions. An apprentice has the opportunity to see the work of the editor up close. The editor may eventually assign some of his or her minor duties to the apprentice, while still making the larger decisions. After a few years the apprentice may be promoted to editor or may apply for a position as a film or television editor at other studios.

**Other Requirements**
You should be able to work cooperatively with other creative people when editing a project. You should remain open to suggestions and guidance, while also maintaining your confidence and holding your own opinion in the presence of other professionals. A successful editor has an understanding of the history of film and television and a feel for the narrative form in general. Computer skills are also important and will help you to learn new technology in the field. You may be required to join a union to do this work, depending on the studio.

"You should have a good visual understanding," Steve Swersky says. "You need to be able to tell a story, and be aware of everything that's going on in a frame."

## EXPLORING

Many high schools have film clubs, and some have cable television stations affiliated with the school district. Often school-run television channels give students the opportunity to create and edit short programs.

One of the best ways to prepare for a career as a film or television editor is to read widely. In reading literature, you will develop your understanding of the different ways in which stories can be presented. You should be familiar with all different kinds of film and television projects, including documentaries, short films, feature films, TV shows, and commercials. See as many different projects as you can and study them, paying close attention to the decisions the editors made in piecing together the scenes.

Large television stations and film companies occasionally have volunteers or student interns. Most people in the industry start out doing minor tasks helping with production. These production assistants get the opportunity to see all of the professionals at work. By working closely with an editor, a production assistant can learn television or film operations as well as specific editing techniques.

## EMPLOYERS

Approximately 21,000 film and television editors are employed in the United States. Some film or television editors work primarily with news programs, documentaries, or special features. They may develop ongoing working relationships with directors or producers who hire them from one project to another. Many editors who have worked for a studio or postproduction company for several years often become independent contractors. These editors offer their services on a per-job basis to producers of commercials and films, negotiate their own fees, and typically purchase or lease their own editing equipment.

## STARTING OUT

Because of the glamour associated with film and television work, this is a popular field that can be very difficult to break into. With a minimum of a high school diploma or a degree from a two-year college, you can apply for entry-level jobs in many film or television studios, but these jobs won't be editing positions. Most studios will not consider people for film or television editor positions without a bachelor's degree or several years of on-the-job experience.

One way to get on-the-job experience is to complete an apprenticeship in editing. However, in some cases, you won't be eligible for an apprenticeship unless you are a current employee of the studio. Therefore, start out by applying to as many film and television studios as possible and take an entry-level position, even if it's not in the editing department. Having a foot in the door at a studio will enable you to make contacts and network as you work towards your long-term goal of working as an editor.

Those who have completed bachelor's or master's degrees have typically gained hands-on experience through school projects. Another benefit of going to school is that contacts that you make while in school, both through your school's career services office and alumni, can be a valuable resource when you look for your first job. Your school's career services office may also have listings of job openings. Some studio work is union regulated. Therefore you may also want to contact union locals to find out about job requirements and openings.

## ADVANCEMENT

Once film and television editors have secured employment in their field, their advancement comes with further experience and greater recognition. Some film and television editors develop good working relationships with directors or producers. These editors may be willing to leave the security of a studio job for the possibility of working one-on-one with the director or producer on a project. These opportunities often provide editors with the autonomy they may not get in their regular jobs. Some are willing to take a pay cut to work on a project they feel is important.

Some film and television editors choose to stay at their studios and advance through seniority to editing positions with higher salaries. They may be able to negotiate better benefits packages or to choose the projects they will work on. They may also choose which directors they wish to work with. In larger studios, editors may train and supervise staffs of less experienced or apprentice editors.

"I want to continue doing films," Steve Swersky says. "Every film is a step up the ladder on the long way to the top." He plans to continue to work on commercials, but would also like to work on films with bigger budgets and more prestige. "I'd like to be at the Academy Awards someday," Swersky says, "accepting the Oscar for film editing."

Some sound editors may wish to broaden their skills by working as general film editors. Some film editors may, on the other hand, choose to specialize in sound effects, music, or some other editorial area. Some editors who work in television may move to motion pictures or may move from working on commercials or television series to movies.

## EARNINGS

Film and television editors are not as highly paid as others working in their industry. They have less clout than directors or producers, but they have more authority in the production of a project than many other film technicians. According to the U.S. Department of Labor, the median annual wage for film and television editors was $47,870 in 2007. A small percentage of film editors earn less than $24,270 a year, while some earn more than $113,580. The most experienced and sought-after film editors can command much higher salaries.

Benefits for full-time workers include vacation and sick time, health, and sometimes dental, insurance, and pension or 401(k) plans. Self-employed editors must provide their own benefits.

## WORK ENVIRONMENT

Editors work in film or television studios or at postproduction companies. The working environment is often a small studio office cramped full of editing equipment. Working hours vary widely depending on the project. During the filming of a commercial, for instance, editors may be required to work overtime, at night, or on weekends to finish the project by an assigned date. Many feature-length films are kept on tight production schedules.

"As stressful as the work can be," Steve Swersky says, "we joke around that it's not like having a real job. Every day is a fun day."

During filming, editors may be asked to be on hand at the filming location. Locations may be outdoors or in other cities, and travel is occasionally required. More often, however, the film or television editor works in the studio.

Disadvantages of the job involve the editor's low rank on the totem pole of film or television industry jobs. However, most editors feel that this is outweighed by the honor of working on exciting television or movie projects.

## OUTLOOK

The outlook for film and television editors is good. The growth of cable television and an increase in the number of independent film studios will translate into greater demand for editors. This will also force the largest studios to offer more competitive salaries in order to attract the best film and television editors. The U.S. Department of Labor predicts that employment for film and television editors will grow about as fast as the average for all occupations through 2016. The digital revolution will greatly affect the editing process. Editors will work much more closely with special effects houses in putting together projects. When using more visual and sound effects, film and television editors will have to edit scenes with an eye towards the special effects that will be added. Digital editing systems are also available for home computers. Users can feed their own digital video into their computers, edit the material, and add their own special effects and titles. In 1999, *The Celebration,* a Danish film made with a low budget and shot with a home digital video camera, won the New York and Los Angeles film critics awards for best foreign film. Advances in film technology may provide some editors with more direct routes into the industry, but the majority of editors will have to follow traditional routes, obtaining years of hands-on experience to advance in their career.

## FOR MORE INFORMATION

*The ACE features some career and education information for film and television editors on its Web site, along with information about internship opportunities and sample articles from* CinemaEditor *magazine.*

**American Cinema Editors (ACE)**
100 Universal City Plaza
Building 2282, Room 190
Universal City, CA 91608-1002
Tel: 818-777-2900
Email: amercinema@earthlink.net
http://www.ace-filmeditors.org

*For information about the AFI Conservatory's master of fine arts in editing and to read interviews with professionals, visit the AFI Web site.*

**American Film Institute (AFI)**
2021 North Western Avenue
Los Angeles, CA 90027-1625
Tel: 323-856-7600
http://www.afi.com

*This union counts film and television production workers among its craft members. For education and training information, contact*

**International Alliance of Theatrical Stage Employees, Moving Picture Technicians, Artists and Allied Crafts of the United States, Its Territories and Canada (IATSE)**
1430 Broadway, 20th Floor
New York, NY 10018-3348
Tel: 212-730-1770
http://www.iatse-intl.org

*For information on NATAS scholarships and to read articles from* Television Quarterly, *the organization's official journal, visit the NATAS Web site.*

**National Academy of Television Arts and Sciences (NATAS)**
111 West 57th Street, Suite 600
New York, NY 10019-2211
Tel: 212-586-8424
http://www.emmyonline.org

# Food Photographers

## QUICK FACTS

**School Subjects**
Art
Family and consumer science

**Personal Skills**
Artistic
Mechanical/manipulative

**Work Environment**
Indoors and outdoors
Primarily multiple locations

**Minimum Education Level**
Some postsecondary training

**Salary Range**
$16,170 to $27,720 to
$59,890+

**Certification or Licensing**
Voluntary

**Outlook**
About as fast as the average

**DOT**
143

**GOE**
01.08.01

**NOC**
5221

**O*NET-SOC**
27-4021.00, 27-4021.01,
27-4021.02

## OVERVIEW

Have you ever seen a picture that made your mouth water? Images like these are the creations of skilled *food photographers*. These artists work hard to make their viewers crave a dish without the help of the food's appealing presence, aroma, and texture. Food photographers create beautiful and enticing images of food for magazines, cookbooks, and restaurant promotional materials. They work with *food stylists* to make the food look as appetizing and aesthetically beautiful as possible. Approximately 122,000 photographers are employed in the United States; only a small percentage of these professionals specialize in food photography.

## HISTORY

Food photography is a relatively recent career path. Only in the last few decades have the food and culinary industries become so huge that skilled professionals were hired for marketing and promotion. Before these changes in the industry, a general photographer might have snapped photos of hamburgers or other basic foodstuffs for menus, cookbooks, or advertisements. Now, a fast-food giant such as McDonald's will spend a large amount of money to hire a large team of food photographers, stylists, and other design consultants to make a Big Mac look perfect. The food must be able to withstand the heat of lights without melting and the passage of time without wilting. Food photographers make their edible models as appealing as possible by using skills beyond those of basic photography.

74

# THE JOB

Food photographers have many of the same duties and responsibilities as other photographers, except their subjects happen to whet the appetite. They must set up shoots with clients and decide on the look of the shot. Once a date is set, the photographer has to make sure all the props are ordered and that he or she has enough help for the shoot. The photographer or the client may hire food stylists, camera assistants, and prop movers to aid in the shoot.

A lot of extra care has to go into the preparation and styling of the food. This is why a separate stylist is almost always necessary for a successful food photo shoot. While the stylist is busy designing the food and placing it on the proper plate, platter, or other background, the food photographer is busy readying his or her technical elements. Cameras, lighting, and props must be arranged and prepared. The photographer is usually the one who decides on the location and other details of the shoot. For example, natural light may look best on some foods, such as fruits and vegetables, but more dramatic lighting might look better when capturing the richness of a chocolate truffle. Lighting for dramatic effect is one of the many decisions that the photographer must make.

These preparations and test shots take time. Because the food may be fragile or affected by temperature, it is not unusual for food photographers to use food *stand-ins*. Once the shot is fully set up and the client is happy with the look, the photo subject, called the *hero dish,* is brought in, and pictures are taken quickly to make sure the food looks fresh and appealing.

Food photographers and stylists employ many tricks to make their food look appetizing. For example, they may use melted wax to keep a hamburger bun on straight or spray Armor-All onto a tortilla to keep it from drying out. All these skills are necessary to make sure food withstands the demands of the shoot.

Many food photographers work as freelancers, contracting work out themselves. Those who do this spend the majority of the time not shooting film, but running their business. They have to promote their business, find new clients, bill clients, pay bills, hire assistants, organize upcoming shoots with clients and stylists, negotiate fees, order and stock supplies, and balance budgets—just to name a few tasks. In other words, freelance photographers are much more than commercial artists—they must be skilled businesspeople, too.

## REQUIREMENTS

### High School

Art classes of all types will enhance your skills as an artist and give you a better eye for detail and aesthetics. Cooking classes will help to familiarize you with your subject matter, specifically how certain dishes can be presented most effectively. Math and chemistry classes will aid your understanding of the technical nature of both photography and food preparation. As a photographer you will have to mix chemicals based on different proportions, edit digital images using editing software, and judge lighting distances by eye, so a math and science background will be helpful. You should also be sure to take computer science classes and explore software that can store and manipulate images, such as Adobe Photoshop and Illustrator.

### Postsecondary Training

Although a college degree is not required to become a photographer, professional training will help you get the experience and skills necessary to land a job and attract clients.

Food photographers often go into one of two training programs: culinary arts or commercial photography. A culinary degree with a background knowledge of photography will ensure that you know your photo subject, including how to prepare foods and their chemical properties that can be affected by shooting conditions. Those who choose to enter photography programs will be well versed in the technical side of photography and may even be able to take some specialty classes in food photography.

Whatever training program you choose, be sure to check out the institution's reputation and specialty. Many professional associations, such as the National Association of Schools of Art and Design, accredit art programs. Also check out online resources for listings of schools. (See the end of this article for sites to explore.)

### Certification or Licensing

The Professional Photographic Certification Commission, which is affiliated with Professional Photographers of America, offers certification to general photographers. Visit http://certifiedphotographer. com for more information. Although certification is not required to work as a food photographer, it can provide you with an advantage when you are looking for jobs.

### Other Requirements

To be successful in their line of work, food photographers have to be patient. Shoots can take hours or even days, depending on the size of the project. An eye for detail is also important to be able to scrutinize a subject for any imperfections that may be imperceptible to the eye but appear on film. Food photographers have to be creative in their work. Some clients will want straightforward images of their food, such as photos found in menus or cookbooks. Other clients may want unique, unpredictable pictures (such as a spicy fajita on a bed of snow) to create a fresh and memorable image of their food. Finally, these photographers should be passionate not only about photography, but also about food. Spending eight hours a day trying to make a salad look just right is not for everyone. Those who can see the potential beauty in average food items—even something as ordinary as a tomato slice—will be the most successful and happy in this work.

## EXPLORING

While in high school, be sure to get involved in clubs that will help you explore your interests and skills in cooking and photography. Most schools have a yearbook or newspaper that you can join as staff photographer. Also check to see if there is a cooking club that you can join in addition to taking home economics classes.

You can also explore this job outside of school. If you have a camera and some film, you have enough tools to explore. Take test shots of kitchen and food items, paying attention to how different lighting and props affect the end result of the picture. Show your pictures to your friends and family and ask their opinion about your work. Does it make them hungry? Do they want to ransack the fridge after looking at your picture? If so, you might be on to something.

## EMPLOYERS

Approximately 122,000 photographers work in the United States, and more than half of them are self-employed. Many food photographers contract their work out with stock photo agencies, which sell photos to large publishers and other companies for general use. Others are hired by food manufacturers, cookbook publishers, food magazines, and restaurants, either full time or on a contract basis.

## STARTING OUT

Because it can be hard to find a full-time job or to start working on your own right out of school, most new food photographers choose to work as camera or food styling assistants. In this position, you acquire hand-on experience with the job and make professional contacts for use later in your career. Some photographers never even end up becoming full-fledged photographers, but choose to continue to work as assistants for better paying or more prestigious photographers.

Again, though a photography or culinary degree is not required to work in this job, formal education will make it easier to break into the industry and attract clients. Having a degree will serve as a measure of your skills.

## ADVANCEMENT

Food photographers can advance in their careers by moving from working for someone else to owning their own business. They may also advance by increasing their client base and working for more prestigious magazines, publishers, or companies.

## EARNINGS

Earnings vary widely for photographers. The U.S. Bureau of Labor Statistics reports that salaried photographers earned median annual salaries of $27,720 in 2007. Salaries ranged from less than $16,170 to more than $59,890.

Freelance photographers have the ability to earn much more than their salaried counterparts because there is no limit to how many clients they may have or how many projects they may be working on at one time. However, commercial and food photography are very competitive fields, so earnings could vary from $0 to $500,000 depending on an individual's business savvy and professional contacts.

Salaried food photographers usually receive benefits such as vacation days, sick leave, health and life insurance, and a savings and pension program. Self-employed photographers must provide their own benefits.

## WORK ENVIRONMENT

Food photographers spend time in their own studio, which is generally well lit and ventilated, especially if the professional develops and prints his or her own pictures. Photo chemicals used in developing and printing can be harsh to work with, but gloves and tongs should prevent the chemicals from irritating the photographer's skin. The growing popularity of digital photography has reduced photographers' exposure to these chemicals, however. When shooting, the photographer may work in the studio or may travel to off-site locations.

Flexibility is key in this line of work. Hours can vary depending on project deadlines, and food photographers may not always have steady work.

# OUTLOOK

According to the U.S. Department of Labor, employment of photographers will increase about as fast as the average for all occupations through 2016. The outlook is also good for food photographers. Their job depends on the overall health of the food and entertainment industries. Though many companies have reduced their advertising budgets, they still have to employ professionals to capture images of their food for print and Web advertising. Most restaurants, no matter how successful, will need to display their food in menus or ads to attract diners.

It is important to note, however, that although there will always be jobs for food photographers, the field is incredibly competitive. Only those with the right blend of technical and business skills will be able to find enough work to shoot pictures full time.

The digital revolution that has hit the photography field has not yet diminished the need for food photographers. This will only mean that food photographers will need to be educated and skilled in the use of these digital tools as well as manual cameras.

# FOR MORE INFORMATION

*The ASMP promotes the rights of photographers, educates its members in business practices, and promotes high standards of ethics.*
**American Society of Media Photographers (ASMP)**
150 North Second Street
Philadelphia, PA 19106-1912
Tel: 215-451-2767
http://www.asmp.org

*For information on culinary education and degrees in food styling, contact*
**Culinary Institute of America**
1946 Campus Drive
Hyde Park, NY 12538-1499
Tel: 800-CULINARY
http://www.ciachef.edu

*For information on accredited art programs, contact*
**National Association of Schools of Art and Design**
11250 Roger Bacon Drive, Suite 21
Reston, VA 20190-5248
Tel: 703-437-0700

Email: info@arts-accredit.org
http://nasad.arts-accredit.org

*This organization provides training, publishes its own magazine, and offers various services for its members.*
**Professional Photographers of America**
229 Peachtree Street, NE, Suite 2200
Atlanta, GA 30303-1601
Tel: 800-786-6277
Email: csc@ppa.com
http://www.ppa.com

*Check out the following Web sites for more information on food and photography careers and educational opportunities:*
**Cookingschools.com**
http://www.cookingschools.com

**Photographyschools.com**
http://www.photographyschools.com

# Graphic Designers

## OVERVIEW

*Graphic designers* are practical artists whose creations are intended to express ideas, convey information, or draw attention to a product. They design a wide variety of materials including advertisements, marketing materials, displays, packaging, signs, computer graphics and games, book and magazine covers and interiors, animated characters, and company logos to fit the needs and preferences of their various clients. There are approximately 261,000 graphic designers employed in the United States.

## HISTORY

The challenge of combining beauty, function, and technology in whatever form has preoccupied artisans throughout history. Graphic design work has been used to create products and promote commerce for as long as people have used symbols, pictures, and typography to communicate ideas.

Graphic design grew alongside the growth of print media (newspapers, magazines, catalogs, and advertising). Typically, the graphic designer would sketch several rough drafts of the layout of pictures and words. After one of the drafts was approved, the designer would complete a final layout including detailed type and artwork specifications. The words were sent to a typesetter and the artwork assigned to an illustrator. When the final pieces were returned, the designer or a keyline and paste-up artist would adhere them with rubber cement or wax to an illustration board. Different colored items were placed on acetate overlays. This camera-ready art was now ready to be sent to a printer for photographing and reproduction.

Computer technology has revolutionized the way many graphic designers do their work. Today it is possible to be a successful graphic designer even if you can't draw more than simple stick figures. Graphic designers are now able to draw, color, and revise the many different images they work with using computers. They can choose typefaces, size type, and place images without having to manually align them on the page using a T square and triangle. Computer graphics enable graphic designers to work more quickly, since details like size, shape, and color are easy to change.

Graphics design programs are continually revised and improved, moving more and more design work from the artist's table to the computer mousepad and graphics tablet. As computer technology continues to advance in the areas of graphics and multimedia, more designers will have to know how to work with virtual reality applications.

## THE JOB

Graphic designers are not primarily fine artists, although they may be highly skilled at drawing or painting. Most designs commissioned to graphic designers involve both artwork and copy (words). Thus, the designer must not only be familiar with the wide range of art media (photography, drawing, painting, collage, etc.) and styles, but he or she must also be familiar with a wide range of typefaces and know how to manipulate them for the right effect. Because design tends to change in a similar way to fashion, designers must keep up to date with the latest trends. At the same time, they must be well grounded in more traditional, classic designs.

Graphic designers can work as *in-house designers* for a particular company, as *staff designers* for a graphic design firm, or as *freelance designers* working for themselves. Some designers specialize in designing advertising materials or packaging. Others focus on corporate identity materials such as company stationery and logos. Some work mainly for publishers, designing book and magazine covers and page layouts. Some work in the area of computer graphics, creating still or animated graphics for computer software, videos, or motion pictures. A highly specialized type of graphic designer, the *environmental graphic designer,* designs large outdoor signs. Depending on the project's requirements, some graphic designers work exclusively on the computer, while others may use both the computer and drawings or paintings created by hand.

Whatever the specialty and whatever their medium, all graphic designers take a similar approach to a project, whether it is for an entirely new design or for a variation on an existing one. Graphic designers begin by determining the needs and preferences of clients and potential users, buyers, or viewers.

For example, if a graphic designer is working on a company logo, he or she will likely meet with company representatives to discuss such points as how and where the company is going to use the logo and what size, color, and shape preferences company executives might have. Project budgets must be respected: A design that may be perfect in every way but that is too costly to reproduce is basically useless. Graphic designers may need to compare their ideas with similar ones from other companies and analyze the image they project. They must have a good knowledge of how various colors, shapes, and layouts affect the viewer psychologically.

After a plan has been conceived and the details worked out, the graphic designer does some preliminary designs (generally two or three) to present to the client for approval. The client may reject the preliminary designs entirely and request a new one, or he or she may ask the designer to make alterations. The designer then goes back to the drawing board to attempt a new design or make the requested changes. This process continues until the client approves the design.

Once a design has been approved, the graphic designer prepares the piece for professional reproduction, or printing. The printer may require what is called a mechanical, in which the artwork and copy are arranged on a white board just as it is to be photographed, or the designer may be asked to submit an electronic copy of the design. Either way, designers must have a good understanding of the printing process, including color separation, paper properties, and halftone (photograph) reproduction.

## REQUIREMENTS

### High School
While in high school, take any art and design courses that are available. Computer classes are also helpful, particularly those that teach page layout programs or art and photography manipulation programs. Working on the school newspaper or yearbook can provide valuable design experience. You could also volunteer to design flyers or posters for school events.

### Postsecondary Training
More graphic designers are recognizing the value of formal training; at least two out of three people entering the field today have a college degree or some college education. About 250 colleges and art schools offer art and graphic design programs that are accredited by the National Association of Schools of Art and Design. At many schools, graphic design students must take a year of basic art and design courses before being accepted into the bachelor's degree program. In addition, applicants to the bachelor's degree programs in

graphic arts may be asked to submit samples of their work to prove artistic ability. Many schools and employers depend on samples, or portfolios, to evaluate the applicants' skills in graphic design.

Many programs increasingly emphasize the importance of using computers for design work. Computer proficiency will be very important in the years to come. Interested individuals should select an academic program that incorporates computer training into the curriculum, or train themselves on their own.

A bachelor of fine arts program at a four-year college or university may include courses such as principles of design, art and art history, painting, sculpture, mechanical and architectural drawing, architecture, computer design, basic engineering, fashion designing and sketching, garment construction, and textiles. Such degrees are desirable but not always necessary for obtaining a position as a graphic designer.

## Other Requirements

As with all artists, graphic designers need a degree of artistic talent, creativity, and imagination. They must be sensitive to beauty, have an eye for detail, and have a strong sense of color, balance, and proportion. Much of these qualities come naturally to potential graphic designers, but skills can be developed and improved through training, both on the job and in professional schools, colleges, and universities.

More and more graphic designers need solid computer skills and working knowledge of several of the common drawing, image editing, and page layout programs. Graphic design can be done on both Macintosh systems and on PCs; in fact, many designers have both types of computers in their studios.

With or without specialized education, graphic designers seeking employment should have a good portfolio containing samples of their best work. The graphic designer's portfolio is extremely important and can make a difference when an employer must choose between two otherwise equally qualified candidates.

A period of on-the-job training is expected for all beginning designers. The length of time it takes to become fully qualified as a graphic designer may run from one to three years, depending on prior education and experience, as well as innate talent.

## EXPLORING

If you are interested in a career in graphic design, there are a number of ways to find out whether you have the talent, ambition, and perseverance to succeed in the field. Take as many art and design courses as possible while still in high school and become proficient at working on computers. To get an insider's view of various design occupations, you could enlist the help of art teachers or school guidance counselors to make arrangements to tour design firms and interview designers.

While in school, seek out practical experience by participating in school and community projects that call for design talents. These might include such activities as building sets for plays, setting up exhibits, planning seasonal and holiday displays, and preparing programs and other printed materials. If you are interested in publication design, work on the school newspaper or yearbook is invaluable.

Part-time and summer jobs are excellent ways to become familiar with the day-to-day requirements of a design job and gain some basic related experience. Possible places of employment include design studios, design departments in advertising agencies and manufacturing companies, department and furniture stores, flower shops, workshops that produce ornamental items, and museums. Museums also use a number of volunteer workers. Inexperienced people are often employed as sales, clerical, or general assistants; those with a little more education and experience may qualify for jobs in which they have a chance to develop actual design skills and build portfolios of completed design projects.

## EMPLOYERS

There are approximately 261,000 graphic designers in the United States. They work in many different industries, including the wholesale and retail trade (department stores, furniture and home furnishings stores, apparel stores, and florist shops); manufacturing industries (machinery, motor vehicles, aircraft, metal products, instruments, apparel, textiles, printing, and publishing); service industries (business services, engineering, and architecture); construction firms; and government agencies. Public relations and publicity firms, advertising agencies, and mail-order houses all have graphic design departments. The publishing industry, including book publishers, magazines, newspapers, and newsletters, is a primary employer of graphic designers.

About 25 percent of all graphic designers are self-employed, a higher proportion than is found in most other occupations. These freelance designers sell their services to multiple clients.

## STARTING OUT

The best way to enter the field of graphic design is to have a strong portfolio. Potential employers rely on portfolios to evaluate talent and how that talent might be used to fit the company's needs. Beginning graphic designers can assemble a portfolio from work completed at school, in art classes, and in part-time or freelance jobs. The portfolio should continually be updated to reflect the designer's growing skills so it will always be ready for possible job changes.

Those just starting out can apply directly to companies that employ designers. Many colleges and professional schools have

## Earnings for Graphic Designers by Industry, 2007

| Field | Mean Annual Earnings |
|---|---|
| Federal Government | $67,960 |
| Motion Picture and Video Industries | $62,070 |
| Specialized Design Services | $48,790 |
| Advertising and Related Services | $46,990 |
| Newspaper, Periodical, Book, and Directory Publishers | $39,390 |
| Printing and Related Support Activities | $38,880 |
| Other Miscellaneous Manufacturing | $37,520 |

Source: U.S. Department of Labor

placement services to help graduates find positions, and sometimes it is possible to get a referral from a previous part-time employer or volunteer coordinator.

## ADVANCEMENT

As part of their on-the-job training, beginning graphic designers generally are given simpler tasks and work under direct supervision. As they gain experience, they move up to more complex work with increasingly less supervision. Experienced graphic designers, especially those with leadership capabilities, may be promoted to chief designer, design department head, or other supervisory positions.

Graphic designers with strong computer skills can move into other computer-related positions with additional education. Some may become interested in graphics programming in order to further improve computer design capabilities. Others may want to become involved with multimedia and interactive graphics. Video games, touch-screen displays in stores, and even laser light shows are all products of multimedia graphic designers.

When designers develop personal styles that are in high demand in the marketplace, they sometimes go into business for themselves. Freelance design work can be erratic, however, so usually only the most experienced designers with an established client base can count on consistent full-time work.

## EARNINGS

The range of salaries for graphic designers is quite broad. Many earn as little as $20,000, while others make more than $100,000. Salaries depend primarily on the nature and scope of the employer. The U.S. Department of Labor reports that in 2007, graphic designers earned a median salary of $41,280; the highest paid 10 percent earned $72,230 or more, while the lowest paid 10 percent earned $25,090 or less. The American Institute of Graphic Arts/Aquent Salary Survey 2007 reports that designers earned a median salary of $44,000, while senior designers earned a median of $60,000 annually. Salaried designers who advance to the position of creative/design director earned a median of $90,000 a year.

Self-employed designers can earn a lot one year and substantially more or less the next. Their earnings depend on individual talent and business ability, but, in general, are higher than those of salaried designers. Although like any self-employed individual, freelance designers must pay their own insurance costs and taxes and are not compensated for vacation or sick days.

Graphic designers who work for large corporations receive full benefits, including health insurance, paid vacation, and sick leave.

## WORK ENVIRONMENT

Most graphic designers work regular hours in clean, comfortable, pleasant offices or studios. Conditions vary depending on the design specialty. Some graphic designers work in small establishments with few employees; others work in large organizations with large design departments. Some deal mostly with their coworkers; others may have a lot of public contact. Freelance designers are paid by the assignment. To maintain a steady income, they must constantly strive to please their clients and to find new ones. At times, graphic designers may have to work long, irregular hours in order to complete an especially ambitious project.

## OUTLOOK

Employment for qualified graphic designers is expected to grow about as fast as the average for all occupations through 2016; employment should be especially strong for those involved with computer graphics and animation. As computer graphic and Web-based technology continues to advance, there will be a need for well-trained computer graphic designers. Companies that have always used graphic designers will expect their designers to perform work on computers.

Companies for which graphic design was once too time consuming or costly are now sprucing up company newsletters and magazines, among other things, requiring the skills of design professionals.

Because the design field appeals to many talented individuals, competition is expected to be strong in all areas. Beginners and designers with only average talent or without formal education and technical skills may encounter some difficulty in finding a job.

## FOR MORE INFORMATION

*For more information about careers in graphic design, contact*
American Institute of Graphic Arts
164 Fifth Avenue
New York, NY 10010-5901
Tel: 212-807-1990
http://www.aiga.org

*Visit the NASAD's Web site for information on schools.*
National Association of Schools of Art and Design (NASAD)
11250 Roger Bacon Drive, Suite 21
Reston, VA 20190-5248
Tel: 703-437-0700
Email: info@arts-accredit.org
http://nasad.arts-accredit.org

*For information on careers in environmental design, contact*
Society for Environmental Graphic Design
1000 Vermont Avenue, Suite 400
Washington, DC 20005-4921
Tel: 202-638-5555
Email: segd@segd.org
http://www.segd.org

*To read an online newsletter featuring competitions, examples of top designers' work, and industry news, visit the SPD's Web site.*
Society of Publication Designers (SPD)
17 East 47th Street, 6th Floor
New York, NY 10017-1920
Tel: 212-223-3332
Email: mail@spd.org
http://www.spd.org

# Medical Photographers

## OVERVIEW

*Medical photographers,* or *biological photographers,* create photographs, slides, prints, transparencies, films, and computer graphics to make medical concepts easier to understand. They provide images of anatomical and biological structures, as well as surgical and medical techniques and procedures. Their images communicate complex medical or scientific information for use in textbooks, professional journals, and other teaching materials. Approximately 122,000 photographers are employed in the United States; only a small percentage of these professionals specialize in medical photography.

## HISTORY

Images used to depict medical procedures and anatomical parts started out as illustrations. Illustration featured prominently in the ancient civilizations of Mesopotamia, Egypt, and later Greek and Roman civilizations. Drawings depicting biological, zoological, and medical knowledge have also been found among ancient Assyrian, Babylonian, Egyptian, and Chinese societies. Modern illustration began during the Renaissance with the work of Leonardo da Vinci, Andreas Vesalius, and Michelangelo Buonarotti.

In 1625, Francesco Stelluti used the newly invented microscope to create a series of drawings of a honeybee that were magnified 10 times. The microscope became an important tool for illustrators seeking to represent details of biological and medical processes. Other tools used by medical illustrators were parallel bars, compasses, French curves, and T-squares.

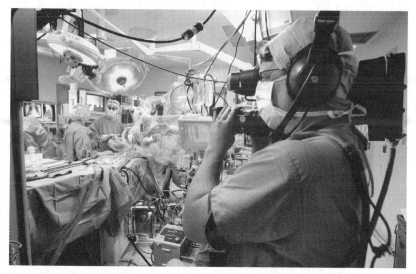

A medical photographer records an operation for a live Internet broad-cast. *(Rhett Butler, AP Photo/The Daily Reflector)*

With the invention of the camera, photographs were soon pre-ferred in the medical world for their accurate and realistic depic-tions. The first medical photography, called photomicrography, was shot through a microscope. The later development of computer technology and the growing sophistication of cameras have made it possible to capture medical processes with complete clarity.

## THE JOB

Medical photographers work in a specialized area of technical pho-tography. They are concerned with representing human anatomy and processes, as well as other biological information. Their work is found in medical textbooks, magazines and journals, advertisements for medical products, instructional films, DVDs, and videotapes, television programs, exhibits, lectures and presentations, and com-puter-assisted learning programs. Some medical photographs are used to create prosthetics and three-dimensional physical models, such as those used for teaching medical procedures.

The role of the medical photographer is to aid in making medi-cal and biological information, procedures, and techniques more understandable. They combine knowledge of biology and anatomy with strong artistic skills.

Medical photographers generally work with physicians, surgeons, biologists, and other scientists. When shooting a surgical procedure, they may observe the surgeon during surgery and ask them for advice about which parts of an operation to capture. Medical photographers shoot parts of the body, such as the eye, the skeleton, or the structure of a cell, for books, encyclopedias, medical product brochures, and related literature. They may also shoot the work of researchers, depicting research on new organisms or drugs.

Medical photographers can vary their style depending on the purpose of a photograph. They often take photos to document patients' conditions before and after surgery, for example. This task requires technical proficiency in photography, but does not call for innovative use of space or lighting in a shot. Photos taken for brochures or advertising materials, however, can be stylized and dramatic. In this case, medical photographers use lighting, camera angles, and design principles to create different effects in their photos.

## REQUIREMENTS
### High School
While in high school, develop your skills in the two areas that are most important in this career: science and art. Classes in anatomy, chemistry, biology, and nutrition will be useful. Aside from taking photography, check out classes in visual design, if available. Most medical photographers use computers in their work, so become familiar with digital cameras and computer art, design, and layout programs.

### Postsecondary Training
Because very few schools offer graduate programs in medical photography, most students obtain an associate's or bachelor's degree in either art or biology. If you are interested in a photography program, visit the Web site of the National Association of Schools of Art and Design (http://nasad.arts-accredit.org) for a listing of accredited schools.

Art classes should cover technical photography, commercial photography, instructional design and technology, and some basic illustration. You will also need at least a basic understanding of the medical sciences, such as pharmacology, anatomy, physiology, pathology, and surgical observation and/or participation.

### Certification or Licensing
Upon successfully passing a written exam, a practical exam, and demonstrating competency, a medical photographer can receive certification in total body mapping from the BioCommunications Association (BCA). Applicants must assemble an extensive portfolio

of their medical photography to complete the practical portion of the certification process.

Additionally, the Professional Photographic Certification Commission offers a certification program for general photographers. Visit http://certifiedphotographer.com for more information.

Medical photographers need to continue their education and training while pursuing their careers. Although certification is not mandatory, you must keep up with the latest innovations in design techniques, computer software, photography equipment, and presentation technology, as well as technological advances in the fields for which you provide images.

## EXPLORING

You can explore an interest in this career by taking art and photography courses. Participation in science clubs and fairs is also a good idea. Potential photographers can always improve their skills by practicing test shots on their own. Visit the BCA Web site (listed at the end of this article) for galleries of award-winning images.

## EMPLOYERS

Medical photographers are employed at hospitals, medical centers and schools, and academic institutions. Laboratories, pharmaceutical companies, publishers of medical and scientific textbooks, and advertising agencies also employ these specialized photographers.

## STARTING OUT

New medical photographers should concentrate on developing a portfolio of their work to show to prospective employers or clients. Most schools offer career counseling and job placement assistance to their graduates. Job ads and employment agencies are also potential sources for locating work.

Photographers can also find job-placement assistance with the Health and Science Communications Association. This professional association is useful not only for job leads, but also for developing contacts in the field and for information on trends and advancements in the industry.

## ADVANCEMENT

After a photographer gains experience, he or she will be given more challenging and unusual work. Those with strong computer skills will have the best chances for advancement. Photographers can also advance by developing skills in a specialized area, such as surgical photography, or even starting their own business.

Individuals who work for large hospitals or teaching institutions can become managers of media and communications departments. They can also teach in colleges and universities at the undergraduate and graduate levels.

## EARNINGS

According to 2007 data from the U.S. Department of Labor, the median annual salary of all photographers was $27,720. Earnings ranged from a low of $16,170 to $59,890 or more.

Because of the technical nature of the work, entry-level medical photographers generally earn $30,000 to $40,000 a year. The field's competitiveness, though, can sometimes lead to lower salaries. Freelance medical photographers generally charge by the hour. Rates vary depending on the photographer's experience and area of expertise. A rate of $100 an hour is not unusual, but contract work may be unsteady.

Medical photographers employed by hospitals and other large institutions generally receive good benefits, including health and life insurance, pension plans, and vacation, sick, and holiday pay.

## WORK ENVIRONMENT

Medical photographers, especially those employed by large hospitals, may have to rush from assignment to assignment during their day. They may be asked to take photos of a complicated surgery in the morning, then shoot pictures at an official hospital event that night. They also may spend time in a darkroom or in front of a computer, looking for and preparing photos for publishing. Freelance photographers travel from shoot to shoot, then typically develop and print their film from a home studio.

Because of the nature of hospital and medical clinics, medical photographers may be exposed to environmental hazards, such as infectious diseases. Like other medical professionals, photographers have to take care to protect themselves from these risks with gloves or masks when necessary.

## OUTLOOK

The demand for medical photographers has declined somewhat in recent years. Cost-cutting measures at institutions have led to increased purchases of stock photography rather than hiring photographers to take original photos. Some physicians also take their own photos, or rely on the media to take them. Despite slower growth, the constantly developing field of scientific information will ensure a continued need for medical photographers.

## FOR MORE INFORMATION

*For information on educational programs, certification, and membership, contact*
   **BioCommunications Association**
   220 Southwind Lane
   Hillsborough, NC 27278-7907
   Tel: 919-245-0906
   Email: office@bca.org
   http://www.bca.org

*For membership information, contact*
   **Health and Science Communications Association**
   One Wedgewood Drive, Suite A
   Jewett City, CT 06351-2416
   Tel: 860-376-5915
   http://www.hesca.org

*For information on accredited photography programs, contact*
   **National Association of Schools of Art and Design**
   11250 Roger Bacon Drive, Suite 21
   Reston, VA 20190-5248
   Tel: 703-437-0700
   Email: info@arts-accredit.org
   http://nasad.arts-accredit.org

# Photo Editors

## OVERVIEW

*Photo editors* are responsible for the look of final photographs to be published in books, periodicals, advertising and marketing materials, or Web sites. They make photo assignments, judge and alter pictures to meet assignment needs, and make sure all deadlines are met. They work for publishers, advertising agencies, photo stock agencies, greeting card companies, and any employer that relies heavily on visual images to sell its products or services.

## HISTORY

For as long as photos have been in print, photo editors have been needed to evaluate them and delegate shooting assignments. In the early days of photography (the late 1800s), the jobs of photographer and editor were generally combined. On the staffs of early newspapers, it was not uncommon to have a story editor evaluate and place photos, or for a reporter to shoot his or her own accompanying photos as well as edit them for print. However, the need for a separate photo editor has become apparent as visual elements have become a larger part of print and online publications, advertisements, and even political campaigns. The trained eye and technical know-how of a photo editor is now an essential part of newsroom staffs and corporate offices everywhere.

## QUICK FACTS

**School Subjects**
Art
Computer science

**Personal Skills**
Artistic
Communication/ideas

**Work Environment**
Primarily indoors
Primarily one location

**Minimum Education Level**
Some postsecondary training

**Salary Range**
$44,906 to $61,182 to $77,459+

**Certification or licensing**
None available

**Outlook**
About as fast as the average

**DOT**
143

**GOE**
01.08.01

**NOC**
5221

**O*NET-SOC**
27-4021.00, 27-4021.01, 27-4021.02

## THE JOB

The final look of a print or online publication is the result of many workers. The photo editor is responsible for the pictures you see in these publications. They work with photographers, reporters, authors, copy editors, and company executives to make sure final photos help to illustrate, enlighten, or inspire the reader.

Photo editors, though knowledgeable in photography, generally leave the shooting to staff or contract photographers. Editors meet with their managers or clients to determine the needs of the project and brainstorm ideas for photos that will meet the project's goals. After picture ideas have been discussed, editors give photographers assignments, always including a firm deadline for completion. Most editors work for companies that face firm deadlines; if the editor doesn't have pictures to work with in time, the whole project is held up.

Once photos have arrived, the editor gets to work, using computer software to crop or enlarge shots, alter the coloring of images, or emphasize the photographer's use of shadows or light. All this work requires knowledge of photography, a good eye, and an awareness of the project's needs. Editors working for a newspaper must be sure to print photos that are true to life, while editors working for a fine-arts publication can alter images to create a more abstract effect.

Photo editors also use photo stock agencies to meet project needs. Depending on the size and type of company the editor works for, he or she might not have a staff of photographers to work with. Stock agencies fill this need. Editors can browse stock photos for sale online or in brochures. Even with purchased photos, the editor still has to make sure the image fits the needs and space of the project.

Photo editors also take on managerial tasks, such as assigning deadlines, organizing the office, ordering supplies, training employees, and overseeing the work of others. Along with copy and project editors, the photo editor is in contact with members of upper management or outside clients, and thus he or she is responsible for communicating their needs and desires with other workers.

## REQUIREMENTS

### High School

In addition to photography classes, take illustration and other art classes to develop an artistic eye and familiarize yourself with other forms of visual aids that are used in publications. Math classes will come in handy, as editors have to measure exactly the size and resolution of photos. To be able to determine what photo will meet the needs of a project, you will have to do a lot of reading, so English and communications classes are useful. Last but certainly not least, computer science classes will be invaluable. As an editor, you will

Photo editors for a daily newspaper in Nigeria choose photographs for the next edition. *(James Marshall, The Image Works)*

work with computers almost daily and must be comfortable with art, layout, and word processing programs.

### Postsecondary Training

While not required, most large and prestigious companies will want editors with a college degree in photography, visual art, or computer science. Employers will also want experience, so be sure to get as much exposure working on a publication as possible while in school. Other options are to go to a community college for a degree program; many offer programs in art or computer science that should be sufficient.

You should also be more than familiar with photo editing software such as Adobe Photoshop, Apple iPhoto, Corel Photo-Paint, Procreate Painter, and Jasc Paint Shop, just to name a few.

### Other Requirements

In addition to technical know-how, you should also be adept at working with people and for people. As an editor, you will often be the liaison between the client or upper management and the reporters and photographers working for you. You need to be able to communicate the needs of the project to all those working on it.

## EXPLORING

To see if this career might be for you, explore your interest in photography and working with publications. Get involved with your school yearbook or newspaper. Both of these publications often appoint student photo editors to assist with photo acquisitions and layout. You should also try your hand at photography. To be a knowledgeable and successful editor, you need to know the medium in which you work.

You could also try to speak to a professional photo editor about his or her work. Ask a teacher or your college counselor to set up a meeting, and think of questions to ask the editor ahead of time.

## EMPLOYERS

Photo editors work for any organization that produces publications or online newsletters or has a Web site with many photos. This includes publishing houses, large corporations, Web site developers, nonprofit organizations, and the government. A large percentage of photo editors also work for stock photo agencies, either as staff photographers or as freelancers.

## STARTING OUT

Photo editors often start out as photographers, staff writers, or other lower level editors. They have to gain experience in their area of work, whether it is magazine publishing or Web site development, to be able to choose the right photos for their projects.

## ADVANCEMENT

Photo editors advance by taking on more supervisory responsibility for their department or by working on larger projects for high-end clients. These positions generally command more money and can lead to chief editorial jobs. Freelance editors advance by working for more clients and charging more money for their services.

## EARNINGS

Earnings for photo editors will vary depending on where they work. Salary.com reports that in 2008, the median expected salary for a typical photo editor was approximately $61,182. Salaries ranged from less than $44,906 to more than $77,459. If the editor is employed by a corporation, stock photo agency, or other business, he or she typically will be entitled to health insurance, vacation time, and other benefits. Self-employed editors have to provide their own health and life insurance, but they can make their own schedules.

## WORK ENVIRONMENT

Editors typically work in a comfortable office setting, with computers and other tools nearby. Depending on the workplace, the environment can be quiet and slow, or busy with plenty of interruptions. Deadline pressures can make the job of photo editing hectic at times. Tight production schedules may leave editors with little time to acquire photos or contract work out to photographers. Editors may have a quick turnaround time from when completed photos land on their desk to when the publication has to be sent to the printer. However, unless the editor works for a daily paper or weekly magazine, these busy periods are generally accompanied by slower periods with looser schedules. A good photo editor is flexible and able to work under both conditions.

## OUTLOOK

Photo editing has been a popular and in-demand field for many years. More and more companies are relying on Web presence, complete with engaging visuals, to sell their products or services. Photo editors will also always be needed to help create a polished look for a printed publication, selecting just the right photos to deliver the right message to readers.

Though computers have revolutionized the way that photo editors work—bringing their work from paper to screen—they have also caused some problems. Improved software technology now makes it possible for virtually anyone to scan or download an image and alter it to any specifications. However, most professional publications will still hire photo editors with expertise and a trained eye to do this work.

## FOR MORE INFORMATION

*The NPPA maintains a job bank, provides educational information, and makes insurance available to its members. It also publishes* News Photographer *magazine.*
**National Press Photographers Association (NPPA)**
3200 Croasdaile Drive, Suite 306
Durham, NC 27705-2588
Tel: 919-383-7246
Email: info@nppa.org
http://www.nppa.org

*This organization provides training, publishes its own magazine, and offers various services for its members.*
**Professional Photographers of America**
229 Peachtree Street, NE, Suite 2200
Atlanta, GA 30303-1608
Tel: 800-786-6277
Email: csc@ppa.com
http://www.ppa.com

*This organization provides workshops, conferences, and other professional meetings for "management or leadership-level people responsible for overseeing photography at their publications." Visit its Web site to read articles on news and developments within the industry.*
**Associated Press Photo Managers**
Email: appm@ap.org
http://www.apphotomanagers.org

*Check out this site to see examples of high-quality stock photos.*
**Stock Solution's Top Photo Site of the Week**
http://www.tssphoto.com/foto_week.html

# Photographers

## OVERVIEW

*Photographers* take and sometimes develop and print pictures of people, places, objects, and events using a variety of cameras and photographic equipment. They work in publishing, advertising, public relations, science, and business, among other fields, and provide personal photographic services. They may also work as fine artists. There are approximately 122,000 photographers employed in the United States.

## HISTORY

The word *photograph* means "to write with light." Although the art of photography goes back only about 150 years, the two Greek words that were chosen and combined to refer to this skill quite accurately describe what it does.

The discoveries that led eventually to photography began early in the 18th century when a German scientist, Dr. Johann H. Schultze, experimented with the action of light on certain chemicals. He found that when these chemicals were covered by dark paper they did not change color, but when they were exposed to sunlight, they darkened. A French painter named Louis Daguerre became the first photographer in 1839, using silver-iodide-coated plates and a small box. To develop images on the plates, Daguerre exposed them to mercury vapor. Daguerreotypes, as these early photographs came to be known, took minutes to expose and the developing process was directly to the plate. There were no prints made.

Although the daguerreotype was the sensation of its day, it was not until the late 1800s that photography began to come into widespread use, when George Eastman invented a simple camera and

## QUICK FACTS

**School Subjects**
Art
Chemistry

**Personal Skills**
Artistic
Communication/ideas

**Work Environment**
Indoors and outdoors
Primarily multiple locations

**Minimum Education Level**
Some postsecondary training

**Salary Range**
$16,170 to $27,720 to
    $59,890+

**Certification or Licensing**
Voluntary

**Outlook**
About as fast as the average

**DOT**
143

**GOE**
01.08.01

**NOC**
5221

**O*NET-SOC**
27-4021.01

flexible roll film. After exposing this film to light and developing it with chemicals, the film revealed a color-reversed image, which is called a negative. To make the negative positive (i.e., print a picture), light must be shone through the negative onto light-sensitive paper. This process can be repeated to make multiple copies of an image from one negative.

One of the most important developments in recent years is digital photography. In digital photography, pictures are recorded on micro-chips instead of film; the resulting images can then be downloaded onto a computer's hard drive. They can be manipulated in size, color, and shape, virtually eliminating the need for a darkroom.

## THE JOB

Photography is both an artistic and technical occupation. There are many variables in the process that a knowledgeable photographer can manipulate to produce a clear image or a more abstract work. First, photographers know how to use cameras and can adjust focus, shutter speeds, aperture, lenses, and filters. They know about the types and speeds of films. Photographers also know about light and shadow, deciding when to use available natural light and when to set up artificial lighting to achieve desired effects.

Some photographers send their film to laboratories, but some develop their own negatives and make their own prints. These processes require knowledge about chemicals such as developers and fixers and how to use enlarging equipment. Photographers must also be familiar with the large variety of papers available for printing photographs, all of which deliver a different effect. Most photographers continually experiment with photographic processes to improve their technical proficiency or to create special effects.

Digital photography is a relatively new development. With this new technology, film is replaced by microchips that record pictures in digital format. Pictures can then be downloaded onto a computer's hard drive. Photographers use special software to manipulate the images on screen.

Photographers usually specialize in one of several areas: portraiture, commercial and advertising photography, photojournalism, fine art, educational photography, or scientific photography. There are subspecialties within each of these categories. A *scientific photographer,* for example, may specialize in aerial or underwater photography. A *commercial photographer* may specialize in food or fashion photography. *Art photographers* use photography as a vehicle for artistic expression. The work of art photographers is collected by those with a special interest in the field, shown in galleries, and displayed in museums of art. *Educational photographers* provide illustrations for books and other publications, motion pictures for specific audiences, film strips, slides, and various other photographic products. There are many other specialized areas of photography.

Some photographers write for trade and technical journals, teach photography in schools and colleges, act as representatives of photographic equipment manufacturers, sell photographic equipment and supplies, produce documentary films, or do freelance work.

## REQUIREMENTS

### High School
While in high school, take as many art classes and photography classes as you can. Chemistry is useful for understanding developing and printing processes. You can learn about photo editing software and digital photography in computer classes, and business classes will help if you are considering a freelance career.

### Postsecondary Training
Formal educational requirements depend upon the nature of the photographer's specialty. For instance, photographic work in scientific and engineering research generally requires an engineering background with a degree from a recognized college or institute.

A college education is not required to become a photographer, although college training probably offers the most promising assurance of success in fields such as industrial, news, or scientific photography. There are degree programs at the associate's, bachelor's, and master's levels. Many schools offer courses in cinematography, although very few have programs leading to a degree in this specialty. However, many people become photographers having no formal education beyond high school.

To become a photographer, you should have a broad technical understanding of photography plus as much practical experience with cameras as possible. Take many different kinds of photographs with a variety of cameras and subjects. Learn how to develop photographs and, if possible, build your own darkroom or rent one. Good experience includes work in picture composition, cropping prints (cutting images to a desired size), enlarging, and retouching. Learn how to use digital cameras and photo editing software.

### Certification or Licensing
The Professional Photographic Certification Commission, which is affiliated with Professional Photographers of America, offers certification to photographers who have had their creative work

reviewed by a panel of judges and passed a written exam that tests their technical expertise. Visit http://certifiedphotographer.com for more information. Additionally, specialized certification or accreditation is available from the BioCommunications Association (for medical photographers) and the Sports Photographers Association of America.

## Other Requirements

You should possess manual dexterity, good eyesight and color vision, and artistic ability to succeed in this line of work. You need an eye for form and line, an appreciation of light and shadow, and the ability to use imaginative and creative approaches to photographs or film, especially in commercial work. In addition, you should be patient and accurate and enjoy working with detail.

Self-employed (or freelance) photographers need good business skills. They must be able to manage their own studios, including hiring and managing assistants and other employees, keeping records, and maintaining photographic and business files. Marketing and sales skills are also important to a successful freelance photography business.

## EXPLORING

Photography is a field that anyone with a camera can explore. To learn more about this career, you can join high school camera clubs, yearbook or newspaper staffs, photography contests, and community hobby groups. You can also seek a part-time or summer job in a camera shop or work as a developer in a laboratory or processing center.

## EMPLOYERS

About 122,000 photographers work in the United States, more than half of whom are self-employed. Most jobs for photographers are provided by photographic or commercial art studios; other employers are newspapers and magazines, radio and TV broadcasting, government agencies, and manufacturing firms. Colleges, universities, and other educational institutions employ photographers to prepare promotional and educational materials.

## STARTING OUT

Some photographers enter the field as apprentices, trainees, or assistants. Trainees may work in a darkroom, camera shop, or developing laboratory. They may move lights and arrange backgrounds for a

# Famous Photographers on the Web

**Ansel Adams**
http://www.pbs.org/wgbh/amex/ansel

**Diane Arbus**
http://www.artcyclopedia.com/artists/arbus_diane.html

**Richard Avedon**
http://www.richardavedon.com

**Margaret Bourke-White**
http://www.lkwdpl.org/wihohio/bour-mar.htm

**Harry Callahan**
http://www.mocp.org/collections/permanent/callahan_harry.php

**Henri Cartier-Bresson**
http://www.henricartierbresson.org

**Imogen Cunningham**
http://www.imogencunningham.com

**Walker Evans**
http://www.mocp.org/collections/permanent/evans_walker.php

**Dorothea Lange**
http://www.mocp.org/collections/permanent/lange_dorothea.php

**Annie Leibovitz**
http://www.pbs.org/wnet/americanmasters/database/leibovitz_a.html

**Art Shay**
http://www.mocp.org/collections/permanent/shay_art.php

**Edward Steichen**
http://www.masters-of-photography.com/S/steichen/steichen.html

**Alfred Stieglitz**
http://www.pbs.org/wnet/americanmasters/database/stieglitz_a.html

**Paul Strand**
http://www.mocp.org/collections/permanent/strand_paul.php

**William Wegman**
http://www.mocp.org/collections/permanent/wegman_william.php

**Garry Winogrand**
http://www.mocp.org/collections/permanent/winogrand_garry.php

A photographer uses the latest in high-tech, mixed-gas rebreather technology to film marine wildlife. *(Mark Conlin, The Image Works/V&W)*

commercial or portrait photographer or motion picture photographer. Assistants spend many months learning this kind of work before they move into a job behind a camera.

Many large cities offer schools of photography, which may be a good way to start in the field. Beginning press photographers may work for one of the many newspapers and magazines published in their area. Other photographers choose to go into business for themselves as soon as they have finished their formal education. Setting up a studio may not require a large capital outlay, but beginners may find that success does not come easily.

## ADVANCEMENT

Because photography is such a diversified field, there is no usual way in which to get ahead. Those who begin by working for someone else may advance to owning their own businesses. Commercial photographers may gain prestige as more of their pictures are placed in well-known trade journals or popular magazines. Press photographers may advance in salary and the kinds of important news stories assigned to them. A few photographers may become celebrities in their own right by making contributions to the art world or the sciences.

## EARNINGS

The U.S. Department of Labor reports that salaried photographers had median annual earnings of $27,720 in 2007. Salaries ranged from less than $16,170 to more than $59,890. Photographers who were employed by newspaper, book, and directory publishers earned mean annual salaries of $37,800 in 2006, while those employed by colleges and universities earned $40,990. Photographers who worked for newspaper, periodical, book, and directory publishers had mean annual earnings of $40,070 in 2007.

Self-employed photographers often earn more than salaried photographers, but their earnings depend on general business conditions. In addition, self-employed photographers do not have the benefits that a company provides its employees.

Scientific photographers, who combine training in science with photographic expertise, usually start at higher salaries than other photographers. They also usually receive consistently larger advances in salary than do others, so that their income, both as beginners and as experienced photographers, place them well above the average in their field. Photographers in salaried jobs usually receive benefits such as paid holidays, vacations, sick leave, and medical insurance.

## WORK ENVIRONMENT

Work conditions vary based on the job and employer. Many photographers work a 35- to 40-hour workweek, but freelancers and news photographers often put in long, irregular hours. Commercial and portrait photographers work in comfortable surroundings. Photojournalists seldom are assured physical comfort in their work and may face danger when covering stories on natural disasters or military conflicts. Some photographers work in research laboratory settings; others work on aircraft; and still others work underwater. For some photographers, conditions change from day to day. One day, they may be photographing a hot and dusty rodeo; the next they may be taking pictures of a dog sled race in Alaska.

In general, photographers work under pressure to meet deadlines and satisfy customers. Freelance photographers have the added pressure of uncertain incomes and have to continually seek out new clients.

Breaking into a specialty field, such as fashion photography, may take years. Working as another photographer's assistant is physically demanding when carrying equipment is required.

For freelance photographers, the cost of equipment can be quite expensive, with no assurance that the money spent will be repaid through income from future assignments. Freelancers in travel-related photography, such as travel and tourism photographers and photojournalists, have the added cost of transportation and accommodations. For all photographers, flexibility is a major asset.

## OUTLOOK

Employment of photographers will increase about as fast as the average for all occupations through 2016, according to the *Occupational Outlook Handbook*. The demand for new images should remain strong in education, communication, entertainment, marketing, and research. As the Internet grows and more newspapers and magazines turn to electronic publishing, demand will increase for photographers to produce digital images. Additionally, as the population grows and many families have more disposable income to spend, the demand should increase for photographers who specialize in portraiture, especially of children.

Photography is a highly competitive field. There are far more photographers than positions available. Only those who are extremely talented and highly skilled can support themselves as self-employed photographers. Many photographers take pictures as a sideline while working another job.

# FOR MORE INFORMATION

*For information on careers in advertising photography, contact*
**Advertising Photographers of America**
PO Box 250
White Plains, NY 10605-0250
Tel: 800-272-6264
http://www.apanational.com

*The ASMP promotes the rights of photographers, educates its members in business practices, and promotes high standards of ethics.*
**American Society of Media Photographers (ASMP)**
150 North Second Street
Philadelphia, PA 19106-1912
Tel: 215-451-2767
http://www.asmp.org

*For industry information, contact*
**American Society of Picture Professionals**
117 South Saint Asaph Street
Alexandria, VA 22314-3119
Tel: 703-299-0219
http://www.aspp.com

*For information on educational programs, certification, and membership, contact*
**BioCommunications Association**
220 Southwind Lane
Hillsborough, NC 27278-7907
Tel: 919-245-0906
Email: office@bca.org
http://www.bca.org

*For membership information, contact*
**Health and Science Communications Association**
One Wedgewood Drive, Suite A
Jewett City, CT 06351-2416
Tel: 860-376-5915
http://www.hesca.org

*For information on accredited photography programs, contact*
**National Association of Schools of Art and Design**
11250 Roger Bacon Drive, Suite 21
Reston, VA 20190-5248

Tel: 703-437-0700
Email: info@arts-accredit.org
http://nasad.arts-accredit.org

*The NPPA maintains a job bank, provides educational information, and makes insurance available to its members. It also publishes* News Photographer *magazine.*
**National Press Photographers Association (NPPA)**
3200 Croasdaile Drive, Suite 306
Durham, NC 27705-2588
Tel: 919-383-7246
Email: info@nppa.org
http://www.nppa.org

*For information on nature photography, contact*
**North American Nature Photography Association**
10200 West 44th Avenue, Suite 304
Wheat Ridge, CO 80033-2840
Tel: 303-422-8527
Email: info@nanpa.org
http://www.nanpa.org

*This organization provides training, offers certification, publishes its own magazine, and offers various services for its members.*
**Professional Photographers of America**
229 Peachtree Street, NE, Suite 2200
Atlanta, GA 30303-1608
Tel: 800-786-6277
Email: csc@ppa.com
http://www.ppa.com

*For information on opportunities in photography for women, contact*
**Professional Women Photographers**
511 Avenue of the Americas, #138
New York, NY 10011-8436
Email: info@pwponline.org
http://www.pwponline.org

*For information about accreditation, contact*
**Sports Photographers Association of America**
c/o PMA-The Worldwide Community of Imaging Associations
3000 Picture Place
Jackson, MI 49201-8853

Tel: 800-762-9287
http://www.pmai.org/content.aspx?id=47742

*For information on student membership, contact*
**Student Photographic Society**
229 Peachtree Street, NE, Suite 2200
Atlanta, GA 30303-1608
Tel: 866-886-5325
Email: info@studentphoto.com
http://www.studentphoto.com

## INTERVIEW

*Jane Shauck is the owner of IRIS Photography (http//www.photoiris. com) in Connecticut. She discussed her career with the editors of* Careers in Focus: Photography.

**Q. How long have you been a photographer? Please tell us about your business.**

**A.** Three years full-time. I run a "boutique" business out of my home as all of my jobs are done on location. My goal for this year is to do 10–15 weddings, 10–15 portrait sessions, and five commercial/editorial jobs. My wedding clients tend to be upper middle class, in their 30s or 40s, are paying for their own weddings, and photography is very important to them. My average client spends between $5,000–$6,000 per wedding. My portrait clients are upper middle class, in their 30s, like a natural, unposed view, and spend about $800–$1,200 average per portrait. I shoot the gala for the 100 Most Influential People in Manhattan each year as Time Inc.'s photographer. I've also shot industrial and jewelry still life, commercially. This year I'm going to leverage my children's portraits into pursuing advertising clients who use children's photography.

**Q. Why did you decide to become a photographer?**

**A.** This is my second career. At 30, I was the sales and marketing manager for an automotive supplier for DaimlerChrysler, and I knew I didn't want to sell headlamps for the rest of my life. I was attracted to photography so I went back to school at night for two years to get a photographic technical degree and then quit my day job and never looked back. It's artistic and emotionally meaningful to me—a great career. And, you can follow your interests with photography.

**Q. What do you like most and least about your job?**

**A.** Best: connecting with people and making them look more beautiful than they think they are, or preserving a memory that will mean more and more as time goes on. Worst: all the editing and administration!

**Q. What advice would you give to high school students who are interested in this career?**

**A.** Don't worry about attending a big name school—it's all about your work and your portfolio—but do go to school to study art and the technical side. Practice, practice, practice. The best thing I did technically was team up with a classmate and on a weekly basis we signed up for the school studio and shot each other in the studio and we would go out and do the same thing on location. Also, shoot weddings as a second shooter—it's like boot camp for photographers . . . all different lighting conditions, portraits, photojournalism, etc.

If you are really serious about getting into photography as a potential career, I suggest you spend the money and join the Digital Wedding Forum (http://www.digitalweddingforum.com). It can answer all your questions and includes the best wedding and portrait photographers in the world. It's also a good place to offer to tag along for free to a wedding, just to get exposure to it. If you prefer editorial photography, join the American Society of Media Photographers (http://www.asmp.org) and go to its meetings. If you want to do advertising photography join the Advertising Photographers of America (http://www.apanational.com) and attend its meetings. Most of these organizations offer student memberships at a lower rate. Doing one of these things will give you such a leg up on pursuing photography as a career and will expose you to the business side. And it will give you access to photographers to network with. I also recommend visiting *Photo District News Online* (http://www.pdnonline.com).

Also, to be a successful working photographer you have to come across as confident (not arrogant). The best way to gain confidence in anything is to expose yourself to everything you are unsure about—technical, marketing, business, etc. and force yourself to take small steps towards your goals. But photography is an entrepreneurial business so you have to practice being a good sales person and a good business person (and it's worth taking some business classes in college while you are there).

# Photographic Equipment Technicians

## OVERVIEW

Photographic equipment technicians, sometimes called camera technicians, maintain, test, disassemble, and repair cameras and other equipment used to take still and motion pictures. They are responsible for keeping the equipment in working order.

Photographic equipment technicians use a variety of hand tools (such as screwdrivers, pliers, and wire cutters) to maintain and repair the complex cameras that motion picture and still photographers use.

As hobbyists' cameras and equipment become more convenient to use, that same equiment becomes more complicated to maintain and repair. Professional cameras—especially those of filmmakers—also have become increasingly more complicated and expensive. In both cases, photographic equipment is too valuable to entrust to the care of anyone but a trained photographic equipment technician. Today, there are approximately 4,400 of these technicians working in the United States, providing services that range from quick and simple adjustments to complicated repairs requiring specialized equipment.

## HISTORY

Although the first permanent photographs were made in the 1820s, it was the introduction of the Kodak camera in 1888 that brought photography within reach of the amateur. This handheld, roll-film camera developed by George Eastman replaced the earlier bulky cameras and complicated dry-plate developing processes that had restricted photography to professionals. The Leica camera, the first 35-millimeter "miniature" camera, was introduced in 1924. It immediately created an immense interest in candid photography and had a great impact on both everyday American life and on the use of photography as an art form, an entertainment medium, and an influential advertising tool.

The early development of motion pictures was also tied to a series of inventions—flexible celluloid film; Thomas Edison's kinetoscope, in which motion pictures were viewed by looking through a peephole at revolving reels of film; and Edison's projecting kinetoscope, the immediate forerunner of the modern film projector. In 1876, Edison presented the first public exhibition of motion pictures projected on a screen.

Further improvements in cameras, projectors, lighting equipment, films, and prints have contributed to making still and motion picture photography a very popular hobby. Whereas early cameras were completely mechanical, modern cameras are computerized, with internal light meters and automatic focus and film advancement. Photographic equipment technicians must be able to repair both the mechanics and the electronics of modern cameras. Digital cameras are the newest development in photographic technology. Film has been replaced by microchips that record a picture in digital format, which can then be downloaded onto a computer.

## THE JOB

Technicians diagnose camera problems by analyzing the camera's shutter speed and accuracy of focus. They do this through the use of sophisticated electronic test equipment. Once the problem is diagnosed, the camera is opened and checked for worn, misaligned, or defective parts. At least half of all repairs are done without replacing parts. All tests and adjustments are done to manufacturer's specifications, using blueprints, specification lists, and repair manuals.

Most repairs and adjustments can be made using small hand tools. A jeweler's loupe (magnifying glass) is used to examine small parts for wear or damage. Electronic and optical measuring instruments are used to check and adjust focus, shutter speed, operating speed of motion picture cameras, and light readings of light meters.

Many modern cameras designed for amateur use include built-in light meters as well as automatic focus and aperture (lens opening) settings. These features are convenient for the user, but the mechanisms require careful adjustment by a skilled technician when they malfunction.

Cameras must be kept clean and well lubricated to operate properly. Photographic equipment technicians use vacuum and air pressure devices to remove tiny dust particles and ultrasonic cleaning equipment to dislodge and remove hardened dirt and lubricant. Lenses are cleaned with a chemical solvent and soft tissue paper. Very fine lubricants are applied, often with the aid of a syringe or fine cotton swab.

Occasionally technicians, especially those employed by manufacturers or shops servicing professional studios, fabricate replacement parts. They use small instrument-makers' lathes, milling machines, grinders, and other tools.

Technicians must be able to discuss a camera's working problems with a customer in order to extract the necessary information to diagnose the problem.

## REQUIREMENTS

### High School

To prepare for this career, high school students should take classes in shop and mathematics. Because digital cameras make up the majority of cameras sold, be sure to take computer science classes to understand how computer chips and other technology can be used to store and download photographic images. Art courses will provide information on digital photo editing. Many camera technicians are photography enthusiasts themselves, so take courses in photography, film, and other art forms to gauge your interest.

### Postsecondary Training

Because their work is highly technical, photographic equipment technicians need specialized training, which is available through either classroom instruction or a correspondence course. Training provides basic technical background information to work with cameras as well as a thorough understanding and working knowledge of electronics. Not all camera models can be covered in a training course. More specialized training on additional models is obtained on the job or through specialized seminars.

Camera manufacturers and importers provide training for their technicians. This training usually covers only the technical aspects of the manufacturer's own products.

### Other Requirements

In order to work with extremely small parts, photographic equipment technicians need excellent vision, manual dexterity, and mechanical aptitude. Those who work directly with the public must be able to communicate easily with people.

## EXPLORING

Larger camera stores often have an on-site employee who does limited camera adjustment and repair. This person can be a good source of information about opportunities in this field. You can also obtain information from technical schools and institutes offering photographic equipment courses. In addition, many schools and community centers have photography clubs, some with their own darkrooms, that offer an excellent chance to explore the field of photography.

## EMPLOYERS

Many of the approximately 4,400 photographic equipment technicians in the United States work in shops specializing in camera adjustment and repair or in the service departments of large camera stores. Quite a few technicians work for camera manufacturers, repairing cameras and photographic equipment that customers have returned to the factory. Some camera dealers have their own in-house repair departments and sometimes hire technicians to adjust cameras on site. Technicians specializing in motion picture cameras and equipment may work for motion picture or television studios or companies renting such equipment to studios.

## STARTING OUT

Individual shops looking for technicians usually notify schools in their area or advertise through national photographic service publications. Manufacturers hire technicians through their personnel departments. Career services counselors at training institutes can help graduates locate openings.

## ADVANCEMENT

Advancement in photographic equipment repair is usually from trainee to worker to supervisor. Many manufacturers' technicians also open their own shops, perhaps starting part time on weekends and evenings. Although technicians who have worked for a manufacturer usually know only one line of cameras well, they can learn other manufacturers' models on their own.

Independent technicians advance as their reputation for doing quality work grows. They must become familiar with all the major brands and models of camera equipment. In recent years, major camera manufacturers have been offering more training courses and seminars to inform independent technicians about their newer models, particularly covering which repairs can be done efficiently in the technicians' shops and which repairs need to be handled at the factory. Because of this increased cooperation, technicians who decide to open independent businesses are now much better able to provide quality services for the types of cameras with which they work.

Some independent technicians expand their activities into selling small "add-ons" such as film, accessories, and used equipment. Some photographic equipment technicians also work as professional photographers during their off-hours.

## EARNINGS

The median salary for photographic equipment technicians was $35,850 in 2007, according to the U.S. Department of Labor. The lowest paid 10 percent earned $18,910, while the highest paid 10 percent earned $58,890 or more a year. Self-employed technicians have earnings that vary widely. In the right location, independent technicians can build up businesses that give them earnings higher than those of technicians who work for manufacturers or shops.

Benefits for photographic equipment technicians depend on the employer; however, they usually include such items as health insurance, retirement or 401(k) accounts, and paid vacation days. Self-employed technicians must provide their own benefits.

## WORK ENVIRONMENT

Photographic equipment technicians work in clean, well-lit shops. They are usually seated at a bench for much of the time, working with hand tools. Eyestrain and stiffness from long hours of sitting are common physical complaints. Tedium can be a problem for some technicians.

Photographic equipment technicians work alone most of the time, concentrating on their work. Patience and steadiness are required to work successfully with the small mechanisms of modern camera equipment.

## OUTLOOK

The *Occupational Outlook Handbook* predicts little or no change in the employment of photographic equipment repairers through 2016. In general, the low price of many of today's point-and-shoot cameras and the high cost of labor make it uneconomical to do extensive service on these cameras. However, as digital cameras have become more popular, technicians able to repair the more sophisticated electronics will be in demand. Technicians whose training has covered a wide variety of equipment brands and models will have the greatest chance of employment.

## FOR MORE INFORMATION

*For membership and general career information, contact*
   **National Association of Photo Equipment Technicians**
   c/o PMA-The Worldwide Community of Imaging Associations
   3000 Picture Place
   Jackson, MI 49201-8853
   Tel: 517-788-8100
   http://www.pmai.org/workarea/linkit.aspx?linkidentifier=id&it
   emid=4544

   **Society of Photo-Technologists International**
   11112 Spotted Road
   Cheney, WA 99004-9038
   Tel: 888-662-7678
   Email: cc5@earthlink.net
   http://www.spt.info

# Photographic Laboratory Workers

## OVERVIEW

*Photographic laboratory workers* develop black-and-white and color film, using chemical baths or printing machines. They mount slides and sort and package finished photographic prints. Some of these laboratory workers are known as *darkroom technicians, film laboratory technicians,* and *developers.* There are 24,000 photographic process workers and 49,000 photographic processing machine operators employed in the United States.

## HISTORY

The first permanent photographs were taken in the early 19th century. In its early years, photography was limited mainly to professional technicians due to many factors, such as the size and awkwardness of early cameras and their accessories, the long exposure time required, and the complex process of developing photographic plates before chemical solutions dried up. However, the Kodak camera, introduced in 1888 by George Eastman, brought photography within the reach of amateurs. This handheld snapshot camera contained a roll of film capable of producing 100 negatives. After shooting the roll of film, people then shipped the camera with the exposed film back to Eastman Kodak in Rochester, New York, for processing.

Further technical developments in photography included the invention of celluloid-based film, light-sensitive photographic paper, and faster methods of developing film. Today, photography has become so popular that there are few U.S. households without at least one

## QUICK FACTS

**School Subjects**
Chemistry
Mathematics

**Personal Skills**
Following instructions
Technical/scientific

**Work Environment**
Primarily indoors
Primarily one location

**Minimum Education Level**
High school diploma

**Salary Range**
$16,330 to $24,940 to
$55,000+

**Certification or Licensing**
Voluntary

**Outlook**
Decline

**DOT**
976

**GOE**
08.03.05

**NOC**
9474

**O*NET-SOC**
51-9131.00, 51-9131.01,
51-9131.02, 51-9131.03,
51-9131.04, 51-9132.00

camera. Professional photographers are constantly experimenting with new ways of creating interesting pictures. While many professional photographers develop their own film in home darkrooms, the vast majority of amateur photographers who use traditional cameras bring their film to film centers, drugstores, or camera stores for development. Photographic laboratories have continued to expand their operations to serve this ever-increasing number of amateur photographers.

The introduction of digital cameras, which store images on the camera's internal computer chips, has brought photography to an even more accessible level. People can now shoot a picture, view it, and then decide whether or not to keep it in the camera's memory. They can then use image editing software at home or at a camera store or photo kiosk to improve the photo and then produce prints or other products. This development, however, has not eliminated the need for photographic laboratory workers since many people still enjoy the challenge and technical nature of taking photographs with conventional film.

## THE JOB

*Film process technicians* develop exposed film or paper in a series of chemical or water baths. Before developing prints, they have to mix developing and fixing solutions. Once chemicals are carefully mixed, they immerse exposed film in developer, stop bath, and fixer, which causes the negative image to appear. The developer may vary the immersion time in each solution, depending on the qualities desired in the finished print. After the film is washed with water to remove all traces of chemical solutions, it is placed in a drying cabinet.

The technician may be assisted by a *projection printer,* who uses a projection printer to transfer the image from a negative to photographic paper. Light passing through the negative and a magnifying lens projects an image on the photographic paper. Contrast may be varied or unwanted details blocked out during the printing process.

Most semiskilled workers, such as those who simply operate photofinishing machinery, are employed in large commercial laboratories that process color snapshot and slide film for amateur photographers. Often, they work under the supervision of a master developer.

*Automatic print developers* tend machines that automatically develop film and fix, wash, and dry prints. These workers attach one end of the film to a leader in the machine and load sensitized paper into the end of the machine for the prints. While the machine is running, workers check temperature controls and adjust them as needed. The technicians check prints coming out of the machine and refer those of doubtful quality to quality control workers.

*Color-printer operators* control a machine that makes color prints from negatives. Under darkroom conditions, they load the machine with a roll of printing paper. Before loading the negative film, they examine it to determine what machine setting to use to produce the best color print from it. After the photographic paper has been printed, they remove it from the machine and place it in the developer. The processed negatives and finished prints are inserted into an envelope to be returned to the customer.

*Automatic mounters* operate machines that cut apart rolls of positive color transparencies and mount them as slides. After trimming the roll of film, the mounter places it on the cutting machine, takes each cut frame in turn, and places it in a press that joins it to the cardboard mount. *Paper process technicians* develop strips of exposed photographic paper. *Takedown sorters* sort processed film.

*Photo checkers and assemblers* use a backlit screen to inspect prints, mounted transparencies, and negatives for color shading, sharpness of image, and accuracy of identifying numbers. They mark any defective prints, indicating the corrective action to be taken, and return them with the negatives for reprocessing. Satisfactory prints and negatives are assembled in the proper order, packaged, and labeled for delivery to the customer.

*Digital imaging technicians* use computer images of traditional negatives (or digital files) and special software to vary the contrast, remove distracting backgrounds, or superimpose photos on top of one another.

*Precision photographic process workers* work directly on negatives. These workers include *airbrush artists*, who restore damaged and faded photographs; *colorists*, who apply oil colors to portrait photographs to create natural, lifelike appearances; and *photographic spotters*, who spot out imperfections on photographic prints.

Laboratories that specialize in custom work may employ a *retoucher* to alter negatives or prints in order to improve their color, shading, or content. The retoucher uses artists' tools to smooth features on faces, for example, or to heighten or eliminate shadows. Some retouchers work in art studios or advertising agencies; others work as freelancers for book or magazine publishers.

Other photographic process specialists are *print controllers, photograph finishers, hand mounters, print washers, splicers, cutters, print inspectors, automatic developers,* and *film processing utility workers.*

## REQUIREMENTS
### High School
Employers prefer hiring individuals with at least a high school diploma for photographic laboratory jobs. Besides photography, courses in chemistry and mathematics are also recommended.

## Postsecondary Training

Many two-year colleges and technical institutes offer programs in photographic technology. Graduates of these programs can obtain jobs as developers and supervisors in photo labs.

## Certification or Licensing

The Society of Photo Finishing Engineers offers voluntary certification to all types of image processors. Contact the society for more information.

## Other Requirements

An interest in photography and an understanding of its basic processes are natural assets for those applying for jobs in this field. Manual dexterity, good vision (with no defects in color perception), and mechanical aptitude are also important. If you plan to pursue a career as a darkroom technician for a professional photographer, you will need to have experience with developing procedures. Film convenience stores and camera stores, which will generally train you in developing and processing, are good places to get experience.

# EXPLORING

Many high schools and colleges have photography clubs, which can provide you with valuable experience in shooting and developing photographs. Evening courses in photography are offered in many technical schools and adult education programs. The armed forces also train personnel as photographic technicians.

# EMPLOYERS

Photographic process workers hold about 24,000 jobs. About 20 percent of these workers are employed in photographic services; 14 percent in the publishing, Internet services, and motion picture industries; and 13 percent in electronic and appliance stores and drug stores.

There are approximately 49,000 photographic processing machine operators. About 70 percent of these workers are employed in retail establishments, mostly in drug stores and general merchandise stores. A few work in the printing industry and in commercial laboratories and portrait studios. A small percentage of photographic laboratory workers are self-employed.

# STARTING OUT

After receiving a high school diploma or its equivalent, prospective photographic laboratory workers usually apply for jobs at photo-finishing laboratories. New employees in photographic laboratories begin as helpers to experienced technicians. As they gain experience, they can start printing and developing pictures on their own. Semiskilled workers usually receive a few months of on-the-job training, while developers may take three or four years to become thoroughly familiar with their jobs.

## ADVANCEMENT

Advancement in this field is usually from technical jobs, such as film developer, to supervisory and managerial positions. Semiskilled workers who continue their education in film processing techniques may move up to developer, head darkroom technician, and supervisory jobs.

Aspiring young photographers often take jobs in photo labs as a source of income while they attempt to establish themselves as professionals. There they can learn the most basic techniques of color, black-and-white, and slide reproduction. Those who accumulate sufficient capital may open their own commercial studios.

## EARNINGS

Median annual earnings for photographic process workers were $24,940 in 2007, according to the U.S. Department of Labor. However, earnings ranged from less than $16,330 to $46,130 a year. Employees who go on to managerial positions can expect to earn closer to $55,000 or more a year.

Most employees work a 40-hour week, with premium pay for overtime. Most salaried photographic workers are eligible for benefits such as medical insurance.

## WORK ENVIRONMENT

Photographic laboratories are usually clean, well lit (except for darkroom areas), and air-conditioned. There is usually no heavy physical labor. Many of the jobs performed by semiskilled workers are limited and repetitive and may become monotonous. The jobs often entail sitting or standing for a considerable amount of time in one place. Employees in these jobs need patience and the ability to concentrate on details.

Some employees, such as printer operators, photo checkers, and assemblers who examine small images very closely, may be subject to eyestrain. Process workers may be exposed to chemicals and fumes and therefore must take safety precautions.

Photographic laboratory work has peak seasons: end of spring (school graduations), summer (weddings and vacations), and the holiday season.

Though the work of developers and darkroom technicians can be technical or tedious at times, their contributions to the clarity and beauty of the finished photographs can be a great source of satisfaction.

## OUTLOOK

According to the *Occupational Outlook Handbook*, overall employment for photographic laboratory workers is expected to decline rapidly through 2016 as a result of the growth of digital photography. Most openings will occur as a result of the need to replace workers, especially machine operators, as they leave their positions.

Digital photography has become very popular among amateurs and professionals. According to Gartner, Inc., a market research firm, nearly 82 percent of U.S. households own a digital camera. As digital cameras and image manipulation software continue to drop in price and rise in popularity, the need for photographic lab workers will decrease. Workers who are skilled in producing traditional prints and other products from digital files will have the best employment prospects.

## FOR MORE INFORMATION

*For industry information, contact*
**PMA–The Worldwide Community of Imaging Associations**
3000 Picture Place
Jackson, MI 49201-8853
Tel: 800-762-9287
http://www.pmai.org

*This organization provides training, publishes its own magazine, and offers various services for its members.*
**Professional Photographers of America**
229 Peachtree Street, NE, Suite 2200
Atlanta, GA 30303-1608
Tel: 800-786-6277
Email: csc@ppa.com
http://www.ppa.com

*For information about certification, contact*
**Society of Photo Finishing Engineers**
c/o PMA–The Worldwide Community of Imaging Associations
3000 Picture Place
Jackson, MI 49201-8853
Tel: 800-762-9287
Email: cpc_spfe@pmai.org
http://www.pmai.org/content.aspx?id=4802

# Photography Instructors

## OVERVIEW

*Photography instructors* teach students of all ages how to shoot pictures, develop film or edit digital images, make prints, and evaluate finished photos. They work in high schools, teaching students the basics of shooting and printing black-and-white photography. At the college level they teach more advanced classes in shooting techniques, color film developing and printing, art history, and digital imaging.

## HISTORY

Though the discovery of active chemicals that make photography possible is credited to scientists, Louis Daguerre, a French painter, is considered the first photographer. In 1839, he developed the first photograph using silver-iodide-coated plates and a small box. The resulting image, called a daguerreotype, took a long time to create and could not be made into duplicate prints.

The process of darkroom photography is generally attributed to the work of George Eastman. In the late 1800s, Eastman invented a simple camera and roll film that could produce multiple images.

With the invention and growing popularity of digital photography (developed by such wide-ranging sources as NASA, Texas Instruments, Sony, Kodak, and Apple), the field of photography is constantly evolving. Those who teach the various processes and techniques of photography must keep up with industry changes while still paying homage to traditional methods and early photographers' work.

## THE JOB

Photo instructors teach photography to high school and college students or to adults in community centers, photography studios, or other settings. They lead class lectures on the technical aspects of photography, take students into the darkroom for hands-on training in developing and printing, and teach students how to edit and process digital images by using computer software such as Adobe Photoshop.

Depending on the nature and level of the class, instructors may limit their classes to lectures, covering technical material such as the relationship between f-stops and shutter speed; how to best capture images in motion, limited light, bright light, or other situations; or how to manipulate camera settings to create different effects, such as a short or long depth of field, blurred images, or high-contrasting images. These instructors are responsible only for teaching within the classroom, and students are expected to shoot and develop pictures on their own time.

Most other instructors incorporate darkroom time into their classes. These instructors teach in the classroom a small percentage of the time, lecturing on techniques and educating students about other photographers' work, and spend the remainder of class time in the darkroom, teaching students how to develop and print their film.

There are three main chemicals, sometimes called washes, used to develop film and print pictures: developer, stop bath, and fixer. Photo instructors teach students how to properly mix and handle these chemicals. The proportions of chemicals to water must be exact, so attention to detail and careful measuring are emphasized.

Instructors also show students around the darkroom before the lights are turned off so they are familiar with the equipment and can access it easily. Instructors show students how to use the printing machines, called enlargers, and how to adjust them to make prints of varying exposure time. Instructors also show students how to take an exposed image (on a piece of photo paper) and put it through the chemical washes so it can be developed and fixed so that it is no longer sensitive to light. At this point, the student can bring the image into the classroom for closer examination.

After teaching students the basics of how to operate equipment and handle the chemicals, instructors teach students how to critically examine their own work to find out how to make improvements or adjustments. They also teach students tricks to salvage a poorly shot image (such as one that is overexposed to light and appears dark in the print form). One of these tricks includes a method called dodging and burning, which either lessens or adds to the picture's exposure time to light and makes it appear lighter or darker in certain areas. Instructors also teach students how to use light filters and other equipment to alter images further once in the darkroom.

The growing popularity of digital photography has changed the types of courses taught by photography instructors. While still teaching courses on the use of traditional cameras and darkroom techniques, instructors also teach students how to use digital cameras. Typical classroom topics include the different types of digital cameras and related equipment, color and alternative processes, studio and location lighting techniques, image editing, and printing techniques.

Besides teaching shooting and printing techniques, instructors also encourage students to be creative and passionate about their work, to study the work of earlier photographers for inspiration and technique, and to keep practicing to imrove their skills.

## REQUIREMENTS
### High School
While in high school, take all the photography classes that are offered. If your school does not have a darkroom, consider taking classes at your local community college or recreational center. Other art classes will also benefit you by broadening your artistic scope and abilities. To be a successful teacher, you should be able to communicate well with your students, so be sure to focus on your English classes as well.

### Postsecondary Training
The level of postsecondary training required depends on where you teach. Instructors working at community centers or private high schools may need only some background in photography to instruct a class. However, if you plan to teach at a public high school, you will need teacher certification and a proven background in photography. If you want to teach at the college level, you will probably need a master's of fine arts degree (M.F.A.) to land a position at a large university. Art schools accredited by the National Association of Schools of Art and Design (NASD) are well respected by employers and art professionals. Visit the NASD's Web site, http://nasad.arts-accredit.org, for school listings and contact information.

### Other Requirements
To teach photography, you need education and ample experience in the technical elements of shooting and developing film. However, you also need to be passionate about the art form to pass the same

feeling on to your students. Students learn at different rates; some will pick up techniques and show talent from the beginning, while others may struggle just trying to load a roll of film or download images from their digital camera. For this reason, you should also be extremely patient and supportive.

In some cases, students take photo classes simply for their own benefit. These individuals are not striving to become professionals, so they should be encouraged in their work and have fun learning the craft. It will be your responsibility as an instructor to create a fun and encouraging climate. In this case, you will need to employ creative and engaging teaching methods.

## EXPLORING

You can explore photography by taking classes or just by practicing shooting film on your own. Even if you do not have access to a darkroom, you can practice shooting images with a basic automatic camera. In this way, you can learn how best to frame shots to create clear or even dramatic images.

To see if you have what it takes to teach photography, try to explain to a friend or family member how a picture on a roll of film becomes a finished print, or how to crop or lighten a digital image using photo editing software. If you can clearly explain the many steps it takes for a negative to become a "positive," or finished, print, or how to edit a digtal image, you are demonstrating good teaching skills.

Another easy way to explore this career is by talking to a photo teacher about his or her training and tips for finding a job. Whether your teacher was trained at a large university or a small fine-arts school, he or she should have good advice to pass on to you about the career.

## EMPLOYERS

Photography instructors teach at community centers, high schools, community colleges, liberal arts colleges, large universities, and art schools. Some photo instructors are hired to work in full-time positions, but a majority of them work as part-time teachers or adjunct professors.

## STARTING OUT

Instructors looking for their first job may find the most luck teaching photography classes at community art centers or community col-

## Books to Read

Frost, Lee. *The A–Z of Creative Digital Photography: Inspirational Techniques Explained in Full*. Newton Abbot, U.K.: David & Charles, 2006.

Grimm, Tom, and Michele Grimm. *Basic Book of Photography*. 5th ed. New York: Plume Books, 2003.

Heron, Michal. *Digital Stock Photography: How to Shoot and Sell*. New York: Allworth Press, 2007.

Joinsen, Simon. *101 Great Things to Do with Your Digital Camera*. Newton Abbot, U.K.: David & Charles, 2006.

London, Barbara, John Upton, and Jim Stone. *Photography*. 9th ed. Upper Saddle River, N.J.: Prentice Hall, 2007.

Long, Ben. *Complete Digital Photography*. 4th ed. Hingham, Mass.: Charles River Media, 2007.

Sammon, Rick. *Rick Sammon's Complete Guide to Digital Photography 2.0: Taking, Making, Editing, Storing, Printing, and Sharing Better Digital Images*. New York: W. W. Norton & Company, 2007.

Schaub, George. *Using Your Camera, A Basic Guide to 35mm Photography*. Revised ed. New York: Amphoto Books, 2002.

leges. These classes are generally open to the public and require less formal training and experience from their instructors. From these positions, instructors can look for jobs teaching at larger schools. If they have teaching experience and certification, they can apply to teach at public schools of all levels. To work at a university or art school, however, instructors need an M.F.A. degree. Those with the degree can get job assistance from their school or through contacts they make in class or in the darkroom.

## ADVANCEMENT

Career advancement may come in the form of higher salary, larger classes, or more prestige. Instructors that become known for their own work can command the highest salaries when teaching because the demand to learn from a "master" will be high. Instructors at all levels can advance by working with more skilled students, teaching advanced techniques and criticism. They may also advance by delving into other mediums, such as computer (or digital) imaging.

# EARNINGS

Earning potential will be largely determined by where the instructor teaches. A community center does not have a large enough budget to pay the same amount as a university. For this reason, instructors can earn as little as $10 an hour or as much as $60,000 a year.

The U.S. Department of Labor reports that art teachers working at postsecondary educational institutions earned a median salary of $55,190 a year in 2007. Art instructors earned an average of $61,000 in colleges and universities and $52,860 at technical/trade schools. In the same year, self-enrichment teachers (including photography instructors who teach at art and community centers) earned a median salary of $34,580. The lowest paid 10 percent earned $18,530 a year or less; the highest paid 10 percent earned $66,470 a year or more.

Depending on where the instructor is employed, he or she may be eligible for health benefits and free or partially discounted tuition for family members.

# WORK ENVIRONMENT

To teach students both technical and hands-on skills, photography instructors work in both a classroom setting and the darkroom. The darkroom contains chemicals that are toxic to ingest and harsh on the skin. For this reason, instructors and students alike must handle these materials with care, using gloves when mixing them and tongs when developing prints.

# OUTLOOK

As long as students remain curious about and interested in photography, there will always be a need for people to teach it. Demand for instructors should remain strong in larger high schools, community colleges, and universities. In smaller schools and community centers, demand for photo instructors will depend on the institution's budget. Photography is an expensive art form because of the high cost of equipment, film, paper, and chemicals. In addition, not all schools have the space for a student darkroom. However, most schools and centers that currently host photo programs should continue to do so and will need qualified instructors to lead classes.

The digital movement that has revolutionized photography will ensure a continuing need for instructors that are skilled in computer imaging and printing processes. Students of future classes should not only be taught traditional darkroom film developing methods, but also know how to download and alter images with computer programs.

## FOR MORE INFORMATION

*For more information on accredited education programs, contact*
National Council for Accreditation of Teacher Education
2010 Massachusetts Avenue, NW, Suite 500
Washington, DC 20036-1023
Tel: 202-466-7496
Email: ncate@ncate.org
http://www.ncate.org

*This organization provides training, publishes its own magazine, and offers various services for its members.*
Professional Photographers of America
229 Peachtree Street, NE, Suite 2200
Atlanta, GA 30303-1608
Tel: 800-786-6277
Email: csc@ppa.com
http://www.ppa.com

*For job listings, career resources, and to subscribe to SPE's expo-sure, contact*
Society for Photographic Education (SPE)
2530 Superior Avenue, #403
Cleveland, OH 44114-4239
Tel: 216-622-2733
Email: speoffice@spenational.org
http://www.spenational.org

# Photography Store Managers and Workers

## QUICK FACTS

**School Subjects**
Art
Business

**Personal Skills**
Helping/teaching
Leadership/management

**Work Environment**
Primarily indoors
Primarily one location

**Minimum Education Level**
High school diploma

**Salary Range**
$21,760 to $34,470 to
$100,000+ (photography
store managers)
$13,624 to $20,150 to
$39,190+ (photography
store workers)

**Certification or Licensing**
None available

**Outlook**
More slowly than average
(photography store
managers)
About as fast as average
(photography store workers)

**DOT**
185, 290

**GOE**
10.01.01, 10.03.01

**NOC**
0621, 6211, 6421

**O*NET-SOC**
41-1011.00, 41-2031.00

## OVERVIEW

*Photography store managers* are responsible for the profitable operation of their shops. They oversee the selling of photography services, repair work, equipment, and accessories. Their duties include hiring, training, and supervising other employees, maintaining the physical facilities, managing inventory, monitoring expenditures and receipts, and maintaining good public relations.

*Photography store workers* assist customers in the purchasing of cameras, lenses, or other technical equipment, or develop film into prints for customers to pick up. They are sometimes called *sales clerks, retail clerks,* or *salespeople.*

## HISTORY

In the United States, small, family-owned photo developers and equipment stores have been around since shortly after the invention of the modern camera in the late 1800s. But with the introduction of the retail chain store, which could buy and sell goods more cheaply than a small "mom-and-pop" photo store, many family-owned stores were run out of business. Currently, national chains such as Ritz Camera (which owns Wolf Camera, Kit's Cameras, The Camera Shop Inc., and more) have grown as more people want to dabble in photography.

These larger retail stores employ large numbers of people, requiring various levels of management and salespeople to oversee the business. Managers are hired to oversee particular areas within the store, such as photo developing or camera repair. Salespeople are also needed to assist customers in the buying of goods and services.

## THE JOB

Photography store managers are responsible for every phase of a store's operation. They often are among the first employees to arrive in the morning and the last to leave at night. Their duties include hiring, training, and supervising other employees, maintaining the physical facilities, managing inventory, monitoring expenditures and receipts, and maintaining good public relations.

Perhaps the manager's most important responsibility is hiring and training qualified employees. Managers then assign duties to workers, such as cleaning and organizing the stock room, maintaining camera displays, staffing the store's digital minilab, repairing cameras, or developing film. Managers monitor employees' progress, promoting some workers and increasing salaries when appropriate. When an employee's performance is not satisfactory, a manager must find a way to improve the employee's performance or, if necessary, fire him or her.

Photography store managers and workers should be good at working with all different kinds of people. Differences of opinion and personality clashes among employees are inevitable. The manager must be able to restore good feelings among the staff, and the workers must be able to work together as a team. Both managers and workers often have to deal with upset customers, and they must attempt to restore a customer's faith in the store if he or she is dissatisfied. Customers who want to drop off or pick up film (or their digital storage units), for example, are often in a rush and may be impatient if they have to wait in line.

Because they deal in high-end, expensive cameras, lenses, and other equipment, photography store managers and workers must keep accurate and up-to-date records of store inventory. When new merchandise arrives, the manager and worker ensure items are recorded, priced, and displayed or shelved. They must know when stock is getting low and order new items in a timely manner.

The duties of store managers vary according to the size of the store and the number of employees. In small, owner-operated stores, managers often are involved in accounting, data processing, marketing, research, sales, and shipping. In large retail operations, however, managers may be involved in only one or two activities. Similarly, workers in small stores handle many duties, from selling cameras to repair work to film developing. In larger camera shops, workers are assigned to work in certain departments.

Whatever they are selling, the primary responsibility of *photography sales workers* is to generate customer interest in the merchandise. In order to do this, sales workers might describe a camera's features, demonstrate its use, or show various models and attachment lenses. Many photo workers, because they sell such expensive, complicated products, have specialized knowledge of camera repair and photography techniques.

Photography sales workers also operate minilabs. They receive digital or analog files from customers, use image editing software to enhance the quality of the images (adjusting for over/under exposure, red eye, etc.), and then produce prints and other related products (such as prints with text, framed prints, greeting cards, and calendar prints). Workers may also process files that customers submit via the Internet or through a remotely located kiosk.

In addition to selling and photo developing, most photo store workers make out sales tickets; receive cash, check, and charge payments; bag or package purchases; and give change and receipts. Depending on the hours they work, workers might have to open or close the cash register. This might include counting the money in the cash register; separating charge slips, coupons, and exchange vouchers; and making deposits.

Consumers often form their impressions of a store based on its sales force. To stay ahead in the fiercely competitive retail industry, photography store managers and workers are increasingly stressing the importance of providing courteous and efficient service. When a customer wants a camera lens that is not on the sales floor, for example, the sales worker might be expected to check the stockroom and, if necessary, place a special order or call another store to locate the item.

## REQUIREMENTS

### High School

To work as a photography store manager, you will need at least a high school education. Helpful courses include business, mathematics, and art. English and speech classes are also important. These courses will teach you to communicate effectively with all types of people, including employees and customers.

Similarly, employers generally prefer to hire high school graduates for most sales positions. Classes in English, art, speech, and mathematics provide a good background for these jobs. Many

# The Benefits of Digital Photography

- Images are immediately viewable on camera; poor shots can be deleted and the photographer gets another chance to create a memorable shot.
- Digital files can be easily transferred to a variety of technological mediums (Web sites, computer hard drives, storage cards, etc.).
- No loss of quality when duplicating images.
- No need to replace film; digital storage cards can be "cleared" and made ready for new photographs.
- More ecofriendly: harsh chemicals are not needed to "develop" photos.
- Photos are easy to edit on a computer.
- Photos can be printed easily.

Source: PMA–The Worldwide Community of Imaging Associations

high schools and two-year colleges have special programs that include courses in merchandising, principles of retailing, and retail selling.

## Postsecondary Training

In retail sales, as in other fields, the level of opportunity tends to coincide with the level of a person's education. Most retail stores prefer managers with college degrees, and many hire only college graduates. Photography, liberal arts, and business are the most common degrees of people employed in this field.

In addition to studying photography, take courses in accounting, business, marketing, English, advertising, and computer science to prepare for a management career. If you are unable to attend college full time, consider part-time study while working in a photography store. This will give you valuable experience while also adding to your education. All managers and sales workers, regardless of their education, must have good marketing, analytical, communication, and people skills.

## Certification or Licensing

The Society of Photo Finishing Engineers offers voluntary certification to all types of image processors. See the end of this article for the society's contact information.

### Other Requirements

To be a successful photography store manager, you should enjoy working with and supervising people and be willing to put in very long hours. Diplomacy often is necessary when creating schedules for workers and in disciplinary matters. There is a great deal of responsibility in retail management, and such positions often are stressful. A calm disposition and ability to handle stress will serve you well.

Retail sales and management work require standing most of the day, so you should also be in good health. The sales worker must have stamina to face the grueling pace of busy times, such as weekends and the Christmas season, while at the same time remaining pleasant and efficient. Personal appearance is important. Managers and salespeople should be neat and well groomed and have an outgoing personality.

Most states have established minimum standards that govern retail employment. Some states set a minimum age of 14, require at least a high school diploma, or prohibit more than eight hours of work a day or 48 hours in any six days. These requirements are often relaxed for those people employed during the holiday season.

## EXPLORING

To explore a career in retail photography, try to find a job in any retail store. The experience you gain in working with customers and handling sales equipment such as registers and credit card processors will be valuable. Of course, a part-time, weekend, or summer job in a photography store would give you the best experience, but these jobs may be hard to find.

## EMPLOYERS

Wherever photography sales are made, there is an opportunity for a sales or management position. In addition to photography retail stores, you may also find employment in large department stores, electronics stores, art galleries, photography studios, small specialty shops, and drug, variety, and grocery stores that offer film developing.

## STARTING OUT

When an open sales position arises, store managers usually hire beginning salespeople who come in and fill out an application. Major department stores maintain extensive personnel departments, while in smaller stores the floor manager might do the hiring. Occasionally, sales applicants are given an aptitude test.

Young people might be hired immediately for sales positions. Often, however, they begin by working in the stockroom as clerks, helping to set up merchandise displays, or assisting in the receiving or shipping departments. After a while they might be moved up to a sales assignment.

Training varies with the size of the store. In large photo stores, the beginner might benefit from formal training courses that discuss sales techniques, store policies, the mechanics of recording sales, and an overview of the entire store. Programs of this type are usually followed by on-the-job sales supervision. The beginning salesworker in a small store might receive personal instruction from the manager or a senior sales worker, followed by supervised sales experience.

Many new college graduates are able to find managerial positions through their schools' career services office. Some of the large photo retail chains recruit on college campuses. Not all photography store managers, however, are college graduates. Many managers are promoted to their positions from jobs of less responsibility within their organization. Those with more education often receive promotions faster.

Regardless of educational background, people who are interested in management should consider working in a photo store at least part time or during the summer. Although there may not be an opening when the application is made, there often is a high turnover of employees in retail, and vacancies occur from time to time.

## ADVANCEMENT

Advancement opportunities for photography store managers and workers vary according to the size of the store, where the store is located, and the type of merchandise sold. Advancement also depends on the individual's work experience and educational background.

A store manager who works for a large retail chain, for example, may be given responsibility for a number of stores in a given area or region or transferred to a larger store in another city. Willingness to relocate to a new city may increase the photo store manager's promotional opportunities.

Some managers decide to open their own stores after they have acquired enough experience in the retail industry. After working as a retail manager for a large chain, for example, a person may decide to open a small photo specialty shop.

Photo shop workers can advance by becoming sales associates or senior sales associates, or they may be promoted to management positions. Again, the workers' experience, competence, and education will determine their likelihood of advancement.

## EARNINGS

Salaries depend on the size of the photography store, the responsibilities of the job, and the number of customers served. According to the U.S. Department of Labor, the median annual earnings of all sales managers were $34,470 in 2007. Salaries ranged from less than $21,760 to more than $60,550 per year. However, managers who oversee an entire region for a retail chain can earn more than $100,000.

Most beginning sales workers start at the federal minimum wage, which was $6.55 an hour in 2008. Wages vary greatly, depending primarily on the store's size and the degree of skill required for the job. Larger photo retailers might offer higher wages to attract and retain qualified workers. Specialized sales workers or camera repairers can make $10 an hour or more.

Many sales workers also receive a commission (often four to eight percent) on their sales or are paid solely on commission. According to the U.S. Department of Labor, median hourly earnings of retail salespersons, including commission, were $9.69 in 2007. Wages ranged from less than $7.11 to more than $18.84 an hour.

In addition to a salary, some stores offer their managers and workers an employee discount ranging from 10 to 25 percent off store merchandise. This privilege is sometimes extended to the worker's family. Many stores also provide sick leave, medical and life insurance, and retirement benefits for full-time workers. Most stores give paid vacations.

## WORK ENVIRONMENT

The five-day, 40-hour workweek is the exception rather than the rule in retailing. Many managers and salespeople work long hours. Managers often work six days and as many as 60 hours a week, especially during busy times of the year such as the December holiday season. Because holiday seasons are peak shopping periods, it is extremely rare that managers can take holidays off or schedule vacations around a holiday, even if the store is not open on that day.

Most salespeople can expect to work some evening and weekend hours, and longer than normal hours might be scheduled during holidays and other peak periods. Most sales workers receive overtime pay during busy seasons. Part-time salespeople generally work at peak hours of business, supplementing the full-time staff. Because competition in the retailing business is keen, many photo retailers work under pressure. The sales worker might not be directly involved but will feel the pressure in subtle ways. Because some customers are hostile and rude, salespeople must learn to exercise tact and patience at all times.

Photo sales workers with seniority have reasonably good job security. However, when business is slow, stores might have to cut some of their workers. Stores may also curtail hiring and not fill vacancies that occur. During these slower periods, competition for jobs and among salespeople to make expensive sales can become intense.

For security reasons, photography store managers must be present if the store is open at night. It is important that the manager be available to handle the store's daily receipts, which usually are put in a safe or taken to a bank's night depository at the close of the business day.

## OUTLOOK

The U.S. Department of Labor projects that the employment of retail managers as a whole is expected to grow more slowly than the average for all occupations over the next several years. Retailers have reduced their management staff to cut costs and make operations more efficient, so competition for jobs will probably continue to increase. Management applicants with the best educational backgrounds and work experience will have the best chances of finding jobs.

The employment of sales personnel should grow about as fast as the average for all occupations over the next several years. Turnover among sales workers is much higher than the average for all careers. Many of the expected employment opportunities will stem from the need to replace workers. Other positions will result from existing stores' staffing for longer business hours or reducing the length of the average employee workweek.

Cameras and other photographic equipment do not lend themselves to self-service operations. These products require extremely skilled sales workers to assist customers and explain the benefits of various makes and models. Future demand will be strongest for photo shop workers who are knowledgeable about photo processing software and particular makes and models of cameras and lenses.

## FOR MORE INFORMATION

*For membership and general career information, contact*
**National Association of Photo Equipment Technicians**
c/o PMA-The Worldwide Community of Imaging Associations
3000 Picture Place
Jackson, MI 49201-8853
Tel: 517-788-8100
http://www.pmai.org/workarea/linkit.aspx?LinkIdentifier=id&
ItemID=4544

*For materials on educational programs in the retail industry,*
*contact*
**National Retail Federation**
325 7th Street, NW, Suite 1100
Washington, DC 20004-2818
Tel: 800-673-4692
http://www.nrf.com

*For information on the photo sales industry, including sales trends*
*and articles, contact*
**PMA–The Worldwide Community of Imaging Associations**
3000 Picture Place
Jackson, MI 49201-8853
Tel: 800-762-9287
http://www.pmai.org

*For information about certification, contact*
**Society of Photo Finishing Engineers**
c/o PMA-The Worldwide Community of Imaging Associations
3000 Picture Place
Jackson, MI 49201-8853
Tel: 800-762-9287
Email: cpc_spfe@pmai.org
http://www.pmai.org/content.aspx?id=4802

# Photojournalists

## OVERVIEW

*Photojournalists* shoot photographs that capture news events. Their job is to tell a story with pictures. They may cover a war in central Africa, the Olympics, a national election, or a small-town Fourth of July parade. In addition to shooting pictures, they also write captions or other supporting text to provide further detail about each photograph. Photojournalists may also develop and print photographs or edit film.

## HISTORY

Photojournalism started in the early 1920s with the development of new camera equipment that could be easily transported as news occurred. A growing market for photographically illustrated magazines revealed a population wanting news told through pictures—and also reflected a relatively low level of literacy among the general public. As World Wars I and II ravaged Europe and the rest of the world, reporters were either handed a camera or were accompanied by photographers to capture gruesome and sometimes inspirational combat images.

In 1936, *Life* magazine was launched and quickly became one of the most popular vehicles for the photo essay, a news piece consisting mainly of photographs and their accompanying captions. Soon, however, photojournalists left the illustrated magazine market for news organizations catering to the larger newspapers and television networks. Less emphasis was placed on the photo essay; instead, photojournalists were more often asked to track celebrities or gather photos for newspaper advertising.

## QUICK FACTS

**School Subjects**
English
Journalism

**Personal Skills**
Communication/ideas
Helping/teaching

**Work Environment**
Indoors and outdoors
Primarily multiple locations

**Minimum Education Level**
Bachelor's degree

**Salary Range**
$16,170 to $27,720 to $59,890+

**Certification or Licensing**
Voluntary

**Outlook**
About as fast as the average

**DOT**
131

**GOE**
01.08.01

**NOC**
5121

**O*NET-SOC**
27-4021.01

The recent digital revolution has changed photojournalism forever. Many papers have pared down their photography staff and purchase stock photos from photo agencies. Some smaller papers might even hand staff reporters digital cameras to illustrate their own stories. Still, photojournalists have a place in the working world, as their trained "eyes" for perfect shots will always be in demand.

## THE JOB

Photojournalists use photography to convey information. They capture stories of everyday life or news events that, supported with words, tell stories to the entire world or to the smallest of communities. Photojournalists are the eyes of the community, allowing viewers to be a part of events to which they would otherwise not have access.

The primary job of every photojournalist is to tell a story with pictures. Photography literally means "write with light," and that is what photojournalists do. They use the equipment that they have to illuminate a particular subject. In order to perform this primary job, photojournalists must be proficient at many secondary jobs: planning, researching, and developing photos.

Before they take pictures, photojournalists need to know the background story of what they are shooting. For example, if photojournalists are covering something sudden and unexpected, such as an automobile accident, they need to know what happened before they arrived on the scene in order to capture the most accurate image.

Photojournalists work with different types of cameras, lenses, and developing equipment and must be proficient in the technical use of that equipment. However, they must also have an artistic eye and good communication skills. While their artistic ability will allow them to capture the best images on film, it is their communication skills that will put their subjects at ease.

Taking photographs is just one part of what photojournalists do. They also write the cutlines or captions that go with each photograph, develop the film in the darkroom, and edit the film for production. For large photo-essay assignments, they research the subject matter and supervise the layout of the pages. Since most newspapers are now laid out on computers, today's photojournalists download or scan their pictures into a computer and save images on disks.

More often than not, photojournalists use digital cameras to eliminate the need for developing and scanning film. Since the debut of the first digital camera designed for newspapers in the early 1990s, digital photography has revolutionized photojournalism. Unlike traditional film cameras, digital cameras use electronic memory rather than a negative to record an image. The image can then be downloaded instantly into a computer and sent worldwide via email or by posting it on the Internet. Although there are still some quality and cost concerns with current digital technology, digital cameras are the wave of the future. By eliminating developing and transportation time, digital cameras enable a sports photographer to shoot a picture of a game-winning play and transmit it immediately to a newspaper hundreds of miles away before a deadline.

Some photojournalists work on the staffs of weekly or daily newspapers, while others take photographs for magazines or specialty journals. Most magazines employ only a few or no photographic staff, but depend on freelance photojournalists to provide their pictures. Magazine photojournalists sometimes specialize in a specific field, such as sports or food photography.

## REQUIREMENTS

### High School

Because photojournalists report on everything from wars to political campaigns to small-town parades, your education should be well rounded if you plan to go into this field. Take classes in English, foreign language, history, and the sciences. Of course, take as many photography classes as possible. If this isn't possible at your high school, consider signing up for classes at your local community college or art center. These classes might put you in touch with other artists in your area and will allow you access to darkroom and computer imaging equipment.

### Postsecondary Training

A four-year degree is recommended to become a photojournalist, although an associate's degree with the right experience is sometimes sufficient. Although some colleges and universities offer photojournalism majors, many aspiring photojournalists major in either journalism or photography and seek out classes and experience in the other field.

Many journalism programs require their students to complete internships with newspapers or other local employers. This is essential to building your experience and getting a good job in this competitive field. Many photojournalists are offered their first jobs directly from their internship experience.

Working on your college newspaper and building a portfolio of your work are just as important as your classes in art, computers, and liberal arts. Another wise idea is to join a photojournalists' organization, such as the National Press Photographers Association (NPPA), for job contacts and professional development. The NPPA offers memberships to high school and college students who are aspiring to study or currently studying photography or journalism. (See the end of this article for contact information.)

### Certification or Licensing

The Professional Photographic Certification Commission, which is affiliated with Professional Photographers of America, offers certification to general photographers. Visit http://certifiedphotographer.com for more information.

### Other Requirements

People skills are essential to photojournalists, as are an eye for art and photography and a working knowledge of camera equipment and computers. It is also important to be able to work flexible hours, write well, and perform research.

Because of the timely nature of many assignments, photojournalists must also be able to work under the pressures of a deadline. They may be assigned to shoot pictures of people in trying situations, such as house fires, car wrecks, or military combat. In these cases, the photojournalist must be extremely sensitive to the people at the center of the story, ask permission to take photos, and when possible, ask for details about what happened. To do this, photojournalists must be extremely tactful and polite and work well under stress.

## EXPLORING

In addition to doing well in your classes, you should also get involved with school clubs that will help you develop writing and photography skills. The most natural fit would be joining the school newspaper or yearbook. See if you can participate on the staff as both a writer and a photographer. If you can, become involved in the caption writing and layout of the publication as well. There is no better way of judging your writing and photos than by seeing your work in print.

## EMPLOYERS

A large percentage of photojournalists work as freelance contractors. Photo agencies and news organizations such as the Associated Press purchase photos from freelance photojournalists to use in print and online publications. Some photojournalists work on staff for newspapers, magazines, or other print publications. Television networks also hire photojournalists to help illustrate breaking stories.

Regardless of where they work, most photojournalists get their first jobs through an internship or professional contacts. The NPPA offers job assistance to its members. Classified advertisements are another way to find out about job openings.

## STARTING OUT

Most photojournalists get their first jobs through contacts made during their internships during college. However, contacts can also be made through professional associations such as the NPPA and other sources. The most important thing that the beginning photojournalist must prepare is his or her portfolio. This carefully selected collection of work should reflect the individual's abilities, diverse interests, and flexibility.

## ADVANCEMENT

Photojournalists can advance by shooting for more prestigious papers (and earning more money for it) or by going into business on their own. They can advance to become the head photo editor in charge of a staff of photojournalists, or they can even become managing editors or editors in chief of a publication.

Other newspaper photojournalists move into magazine photography, usually on a freelance basis. Where newspaper photojournalists are generalists, magazine photography is usually more specific in nature.

## EARNINGS

Salaries vary drastically depending on the size and location of a photojournalist's employer. In general, the smaller the employer, the smaller the salary. Larger news organizations can offer staff photojournalists much more pay and added benefits such as medical insurance.

Freelance rates are dependent on both the experience of the photographer and the size of the magazine, but can sometimes be as high as $800 per day. The U.S. Department of Labor reports that photographers (in general) earned a median salary of $27,720 a year in 2007, with a low of $16,170 and a high of $59,890 or more. That same year, those working with newspapers, books, and other publications earned an average of $40,070, while those working in radio and television broadcasting earned an average of $40,290.

Photojournalists who work full-time for a company usually receive benefits such as vacation days, sick leave, health and life insurance, and a savings and pension program. Self-employed photojournalists must provide their own benefits.

## WORK ENVIRONMENT

Photojournalists work where their stories take them, such as sporting events, political rallies, or even the front lines of war. They also work in photo labs, offices, or out of their homes, developing film, printing images, downloading them onto computers, and writing accompanying text and captions. Because of these varying work environments, photojournalists have to be flexible and able to work under many different circumstances, from a quiet office to a roaring, crowded stadium.

## OUTLOOK

Employment for photojournalists will grow about as fast as the average over the next several years, according to the U.S. Department of Labor. A continued need for visual images in many areas should spur the demand for qualified photographers. Photojournalism is a highly competitive field, but individuals who develop a strong portfolio, maintain professional contacts, and stay on the edge of developing digital technology will find job opportunities in the future.

## FOR MORE INFORMATION

*The ASMP promotes the rights of photographers, educates its members in business practices, and promotes high standards of ethics.*
**American Society of Media Photographers (ASMP)**
150 North Second Street
Philadelphia, PA 19106-1912
Tel: 215-451-2767
http://www.asmp.org

*Visit the NPPA's Web site to see examples of award-winning photographs and to read resources geared directly towards students.*
**National Press Photographers Association (NPPA)**
3200 Croasdaile Drive, Suite 306
Durham, NC 27705-2588
Tel: 919-383-7246
Email: info@nppa.org
http://www.nppa.org

# Photo Stylists

## OVERVIEW

Photo styling is actually an all-encompassing term for the many and varied contributions that a *photo stylist* brings to the job. Primarily, the photo stylist works with a photographer to create a particular image, using props, backgrounds, accessories, clothing, costumes, food, linens, and other set elements. Much of the work exists within the print advertising industry, although stylists are also called to do film and commercial shoots. There are many specialties that can be included on a photo stylist's resume, from fashion to food, bridal to bathrooms, hair and makeup styling, to prop shopping and location searches. Some stylists may focus on one specialty; others may seek to maintain a wide repertoire of skills. While photo styling may seem like a vague and nebulous profession, it is an increasingly vital part of the photography and advertising industries.

## HISTORY

Photo styling has existed since the first photographs were taken. Someone, whether it is a photographer, an assistant, a studio worker, a designer, or an editor, has to make sure all the elements within the frame are arranged in a certain way. Hair and makeup stylists in the film and publishing industries were probably the first to gain recognition (and credit). In fact, most people still associate "styling" exclusively with hair and makeup work, without fully appreciating the contribution of other stylists to the finished photo or film. To this day, photo styling credits are only occasionally listed in fashion and advertising spreads, but that trend is changing. Society is becoming more visually oriented, and the contributions made by stylists are becoming more important. Stylists are gaining the respect of people within the film, television, and print industries. Some photographer/stylist teams are as well known for their collaborative work as are actors and directors. After toiling in relative obscurity for many years, photo stylists are emerging as powerful voices in industry and in society.

## THE JOB

The photo stylist is a creative collaborator, working with photographers, art directors, models, design houses, and clients to produce a visual image, usually for commercial purposes. It is both a technical and artistic occupation. The kind of work a photo stylist performs depends upon, among other things, the nature of the photography; the needs of the photographer, studio, and art director; and the requests of the client. Because these factors vary from one situation to another, it is impossible to list all the aspects of a photo stylist's job. In simple terms, what a stylist does is help to create a "look." The specifics of how it is done are far more complicated. Moreover, *photo styling* itself is a very general term—there are many kinds of styling, almost as many as there are reasons for taking a photograph.

Prop gathering and set decoration are the most common assignments in photo styling, but there are many subspecialties within the field, each requiring different skills and experience. For example, fashion, wardrobe, and portrait shoots often require a number of professional stylists on hand to scout locations, prepare the set, acquire clothes and accessories, dress the models, and style hair and makeup.

*Food stylists* employ a variety of techniques, such as painting and glazing, to make everything from a bowl of cereal to a crawfish etouffee appear especially appetizing.

*Home furnishings and domestic items specialists* often introduce various props to give a natural look to the photographic set.

*On-figure stylists* fit clothes to a model, and *off-figure stylists* arrange clothes in attractive stacks or against an interesting background.

*Soft-goods stylists* introduce appropriate fabric, linens, and clothing into a shoot. The *tabletop stylist* may use anything from glue to Vaseline to give an added allure to a set of socket wrenches. *Hair and makeup stylists* are almost invariably cosmetic specialists, and are usually present on any set that employs live models.

*Casting stylists* locate modeling talent. Other stylists specialize in set design, child photography, bedding, bridal, and catalogs. Many stylists are adept in more than one area, making them difficult to categorize.

Stylists may also bring special talents to the set, like floral design, gift wrapping, model building, or antiquing. They usually have a bag of tricks that will solve problems or create certain effects; a stylist's work kit might include everything from duct tape and cotton wadding to C-clamps and salt shakers. Sometimes a photo stylist is called upon to design and build props, perform on-set, do last-minute tailoring, or even coordinate the entire production from the location search to crew accommodations. The most successful stylists will adapt to the needs of the job, and if they can't produce something themselves, they will know in an instant how and where to find someone who can. Versatility and flexibility are key attributes no matter what the stylist's specialty.

Being prepared for every possible situation is a large part of the photo stylist's job. Knowledge of photographic techniques, especially lighting, lenses, and filters, can help a stylist communicate better with the photographer. An understanding of the advertising industry and familiarity with specific product lines and designers, are also good tools for working with clients.

Organization is another vital aspect of the photo stylist's job. Before the shoot, the stylist must be sure that everything needed has been found and will arrive on time at the studio or location. During the shoot, even while working on a model or set, the stylist must be sure that all borrowed materials are being treated with care and that preparations for the next shot are underway. Afterwards, he or she must return items and maintain receipts and records, so as to keep the project within budget. The freelance stylist does all this while also rounding up new assignments and maintaining a current portfolio.

Only part of the stylist's time is spent in photo studios or on location. Much of the work is done on the phone and on the street, preparing for the job by gathering props and materials, procuring clothes, contacting models, or renting furniture. For the freelancer, lining up future employment can be a job in itself. A senior stylist working in-house at a magazine may have additional editorial duties, including working with art directors to introduce concepts and compose advertising narratives.

Even during downtime, the stylist must keep an eye out for ways to enhance his or her marketability. The chance discovery

A photo stylist prepares clothing for a shoot. *(Terry Wild Photography)*

of a new boutique or specialty shop on the way to the grocery store can provide the stylist with a valuable new resource for later assignments. Maintaining a personal directory of resources is as essential as keeping a portfolio. Staying abreast of current trends and tastes through the media is also important, especially in the areas of fashion and lifestyle.

What a stylist does on the job depends largely upon his or her unique talents and abilities. Photo stylists with the most experience and creative resources will make the greatest contribution to a project. As a premier stylist, that contribution extends beyond the set to the society as a whole: shaping its tastes, making its images, and creating art that defines the era.

## REQUIREMENTS

### High School
A number of classes in high school can help prepare you for this career. Take classes in the visual arts to learn about design and composition. Develop your hand-eye coordination in sculpture or pottery classes, where you will be producing three-dimensional objects. Painting classes will teach you about colors, and photography classes will give you a familiarity using this medium. Skill with fabric is a must, so take family and consumer science classes that concentrate on fabric work. You will be able to cultivate your skills pressing and steaming clothes, doing minor alterations, and completing needlework. Because your work as a photo stylist may require you to work as a freelancer (running your own business) take mathematics classes or business and accounting classes that will prepare you to keep your own financial records. Of course, English classes are important. English classes will give you the communication skills that you will need to work well with a variety of people, to promote your own work, and to drum up new business. The specialties employed for certain shoots require a familiarity with, for instance, food preparation, home decorating, children, formal attire, bedding, and any number of other potential subjects. A photo stylist, like any artist, draws from his or her own experience for inspiration, so exposure to a wide variety of experiences will benefit anyone entering the field.

### Postsecondary Training
There is no specific postsecondary educational or training route you must take to enter this field. Some photo stylists have attended art schools, receiving degrees in photography. Others have entered the field by going into retail, working for large department stores, for example, to gain experience with advertising, marketing, and even product display. The Association of Stylists and Coordinators (ASC) recommends entering the field by working as an assistant

for an established stylist. According to the ASC, such an informal apprenticeship usually lasts about two years. By then, the assistant typically has enough skills and connections to begin working on his or her own.

If you are interested in a specialized type of styling, you may want to consider gaining experience in that area. For example, if hair and makeup styling interests you, consider taking classes at a local cosmetology school that will teach you how to work with different kinds of hair. If food styling interests you, consider taking cooking or baking classes at a culinary school. Again, this will give you experience working with the materials to be photographed. It is essential to have a knowledge of photography for this work, so continue to take photography classes to build your skills. Advertising courses may also be useful.

### Other Requirements
The personal qualities most sought in a photo stylist are creativity, taste, resourcefulness, and good instincts. Stylists work with a variety of people, such as clients, models, and prop suppliers, and therefore they need to have a calm and supportive personality. Schedules can be hectic and work is not always done during normal business hours, so stylists need flexibility, the ability to work under pressure, and patience. Stylists who are easy to work with often find that they have a large number of clients. Finally, an eye for detail is a must. Stylists are responsible for making sure that everything appearing in a photo—from a model's hairstyle to the size and color of a lamp—is exactly right.

## EXPLORING

There are a number of fun ways to explore your interest in this career. Try teaming up with a friend to conduct your own photo shoot. Arm yourself with a camera, decide on a location (inside or outside), gather some props or costumes, and take a series of photographs. At a professional level, these are known as test shots and are used to build up the portfolios of photographers, models, and stylists. But a backyard photo shoot can be a good way to appreciate the elements involved with this career. Obviously, any opportunity to visit a real photographer's set can be an invaluable learning experience; ask a guidance counselor to help you arrange such a field trip. You should also consider joining a photography or art club. Besides giving you the opportunity to work with the medium, such clubs may also sponsor talks or meetings with professionals in the field.

Look for part-time or summer work in the retail field where you may have the opportunity to set up displays and learn about advertising. Even if you can't find such work, watch someone prepare a display in a department store window. Many stylists start out as window dressers or doing in-store display work.

## EMPLOYERS

There are relatively few positions available for full-time, salaried photo stylists. Some ad agencies, magazines, and companies that sell their merchandise through catalogs have stylists on staff. Most photo stylists, however, work as freelancers. They are hired for individual assignments by photographers, ad agencies, design firms, catalog houses, and any other enterprise that uses photographic services.

## STARTING OUT

A person can enter the field of photo styling at any point in life, but there is no clear-cut way to go about it. Some people, if they have the resources, hire photographers to shoot a portfolio with them, then shop it around to production houses and other photographers. However, most prospective employers prefer that a stylist has previous on-set experience.

As the ASC recommends, one of the best ways to break into this field is to find work as a stylist's assistant. Production houses and photo studios that employ full-time stylists usually keep a directory of assistants. Most cities have a creative directory of established stylists who may need assistants. It is important to always leave a name and number; they may have no work available immediately, but might be desperate for help next month. Working as an assistant will provide you with important on-set experience as well as show you the nuts and bolts of the job—including the drudgery along with the rewards. Building a reputation is the most important thing to do at any stage of this career, since most photographers find stylists by word of mouth and recommendations, in addition to reviewing portfolios. Assistants will also be introduced to the people who may hire them down the road as full-fledged stylists, giving them an opportunity to make a good impression. Eventually, you can seek out a photographer who needs a stylist and work together on test shots. Once you have enough examples of your work for a portfolio, you can show it to agents, editors, and photographers.

Agency representation can be of enormous help to the freelancer. An agent finds work for the stylist and pays him or her on a regular basis (after extracting an average commission of 20 percent). The benefits of representation is that while a stylist is working one job, the agent is lining up the next. Some agencies represent stylists exclusively; others also handle models, photographers, and actors.

## ADVANCEMENT

Advancement in this field can be measured by the amount of bookings a stylist obtains, the steadiness of work, and a regularly increasing pay rate. It can also be determined by the quality of a stylist's clients, the reputation of the photographer, and the nature of the assignments. Some stylists start out with lower-end catalogs and work their way up. If the goal is to do high fashion, then the steps along the way will be readily apparent in the quality of the merchandise and the size of the client. The opportunity to work with highly regarded photographers is also a step up, even if the stylist's pay rate remains the same. In a career built on reputation, experience with the industry's major players is priceless. Senior stylists at magazines often help in ad design and planning. Some stylists advance to become art directors and fashion editors. Ultimately, each stylist has his or her own goals in sight. The "rare-air" of high fashion and celebrity photography may not be the end-all for all stylists; a good steady income and the chance to work regularly with friendly, creative people may, in fact, be of more importance to a stylist.

## EARNINGS

Like almost everything else in this field, earning potential varies from one stylist to the next. Salaries at production houses can start as low as $8 an hour, but usually include fringe benefits like health insurance, not to mention a regular paycheck. The freelancer, on the other hand, has enormous earning potential. An experienced fashion or food stylist can demand as much as $800 or more a day, depending on his or her reputation and the budget of the production. Regular bookings at this level, along with travel and accommodation costs (almost always paid for), translate into a substantial income.

Most photo stylists, however, earn less and average approximately $350 to $500 per day. According to the ASC, assistant stylists, who are hired by the day, can expect to make approximately $150 to $200 per day. Neither assistants nor stylists who are freelancers receive any kind of benefits. They must provide for their own health insurance and retirement, and they receive no pay for sick days or vacation days. In addition, while a stylist may have a job that pays

$500 a day for several days, the stylist may also have unpaid periods when he or she is looking for the next assignment.

## WORK ENVIRONMENT

Work conditions for a photo stylist are as varied as the job itself. Preparation for a shoot may involve hours on the telephone, calling from the home or office, and more hours shopping for props and materials to use on the set. Much of the work is done inside comfortable photo studios or at other indoor locations, but sometimes, especially in fashion and catalog photography, outdoor locations are also used. If the merchandise is of a seasonal nature, this could mean long days working in a cold field photographing winter parkas against a snowy background, or it could mean flying down to Key West in January for a week shooting next summer's line of swimwear. Travel, both local and long distance, is part of the job. Days can be long, from dawn to dusk, or they may require the stylist's presence for only a few hours on the set. Hours vary, but a stylist must always be flexible, especially the freelancer who may be called in on a day's notice.

Regardless of whether stylists own or rent photo and prop equipment, they must be prepared to put out a lot of their own money. Most clients and studios budget for these expenses and reimburse the stylist, but the initial funds must sometimes come from the stylist's own pocket. Maintaining a portfolio, purchasing equipment, and paying agents' fees may also add to the cost of doing business.

Photo styling can be an extremely lucrative career, but there is no assurance that a stylist will find steady employment. It is wise to establish an emergency fund in the event that work disappears for a time. Busy periods often correspond to seasonal advertising campaigns and film work. A stylist might have a great year followed by a disappointing one. Freelancers must file their own quarterly tax returns and purchase their own health insurance.

Stress levels vary from one assignment to the next. Some shoots may go smoothly, others may have a crisis occur every minute. Stylists must be able to remain calm and resilient in the face of enormous pressure. Personality clashes may also occur despite every effort to avoid them, adding to the stress of the job. For the freelancer, the pressure to find new work and maintain proper business records are still further sources of stress. Photo stylists will also spend considerable time on their feet, stooping and kneeling in uncomfortable positions or trying to get something aligned just right. They also may need to transport heavy material and merchandise to and from the studio or location or move these elements around the set during the shoot. Reliable transportation is essential.

The irregular hours of a photo stylist can be an attraction for people who enjoy variety in their lives. Work conditions are not always that strenuous. The work can also be pleasant and fun, as the crew trades jokes and experiences, solves problems together, and shares the excitement of a sudden inspiration. The rewards of working with a team of professionals on an interesting, creative project is a condition of the job that most stylists treasure.

## OUTLOOK

The value of a good photo stylist is becoming more and more apparent to photographers and advertising clients. However, the outlook for employment for stylists depends a great deal on their perseverance and reputation. Larger cities are the most fertile places to find work, but there are photo studios in nearly every community. The fortunes of the stylist are intrinsically related to the health of the advertising, film, video, and commercial photography industries—all of which are in good shape. Stylists should try, however, to maintain a wide client base if possible, so they can be assured of regular work in case one source dries up.

Technological advances, especially in the areas of digital photography and photo enhancement, may transform, but not eliminate, the role of the photo stylist in the future. Someday there may be educational avenues for the stylist to enter into the field, and this may increase the amount of competition for styling assignments. Ultimately, though, maintaining the quality of work is the best insurance for continued employment.

## FOR MORE INFORMATION

*For information on the career of photo stylist, contact*
**Association of Stylists and Coordinators**
18 East 18th Street, #5E
New York, NY 10003-1933
Email: info@stylistsasc.com
http://www.stylistsasc.com

*To see examples of professional photography and read about news in the field, check out the following publication and Web site:*
**Photo District News**
770 Broadway, 7th Floor
New York, NY 10003-9522

Tel: 646-654-5780

http://www.pdonline.com

## INTERVIEW

*Kelly McKaig is a photo stylist in Chicago, Illinois. (Visit http://www. kellymckaigstylist.com to view her work.) She discussed her career with the editors of* Careers in Focus: Photography.

**Q. Can you please tell us about your business?**

**A.** I am a prop stylist, which means that I work with a photographer, art director, and other members of a photo team on photo shoots. My role is to help in the selection and provision of props, backgrounds, surfaces, and other random items as needed. I also assist in decisions concerning style, design, color, mood, etc. A large part of my job consists of shopping before the shoot: I need to know what items are available (for example, dishes, tablecloths, furniture, flowers, etc.) and where to find them. I also work on set during the shoot. Set duties include preparing merchandise and props (cleaning, ironing, steaming, etc.), roughing in the shot, tweaking, etc. Styling basically means making the product or environment look good in whatever way it needs to.

Sometimes I am the point person with the art director and give the photographer notes and direction. Sometimes the photographer has a closer relationship with the art director, ad agency, and/or client, and I get my direction from him or her. Usually the photographer hires me, although it sometimes happens that the client hires me directly. I work in print; this includes magazines, books, catalogs and advertising (Sunday circular mailers, billboards, in-store graphics, menu inserts, packaging, etc.). It is also possible to work on commercials (i.e., moving film).

**Q. What is your work environment like?**

**A.** I have a home office and a prop storage area and shoot with the photographer either at the photographer's studio or on location. The location can be (and usually is) a house, although I've shot on a couple of Lake Michigan beaches, in some parks, and at some businesses. Location is useful because it provides resources in terms of architectural elements, indoor and outdoor environments, lighting situations, and props. It does mean, however, that everything including photography equipment, lighting equipment, merchandise, props, food, etc. must be transported to the location. This requires packing everything up prior to the shoot, traveling, unloading before the shoot, doing the shoot, packing everything up again, traveling back, and unloading.

**Q. Why did I decide to become a photo stylist?**

**A.** I have a background in fine art photography. I wanted to keep my art separate from my livelihood, but I also wanted to get out of office work. A friend told me about the job of a stylist and I felt that a job/career where I could use my creativity and draw on my photo background would be very satisfying and exciting. Once I started assisting, I realized that collaborating with a team was something that I enjoyed a lot. I also really liked the work schedule. The days are long, generally 10 hours, oftentimes more. But not every day is booked with work and so there is time during the week to go to the art museum, travel, research sources, etc. The downside to this is that because no work is guaranteed, it can be difficult to justify turning down projects in favor of personal time.

**Q. What kind of educational path did you pursue to become a photo stylist?**

**A.** There are no requirements, per se, although it is assumed that one would have a college degree.

Training for photo styling is done on an apprenticeship model. A person generally begins as an assistant and works for a number of different stylists who, in turn, work for a number of different photographers. This provides a wide range of experience. As the assistant's experience and confidence grow, he or she hooks up with photo assistants or photographers to work on "samples" or "tests," which are personal projects. This is the way the assistant builds images to create a portfolio. After a portfolio comes together (sometimes before), the assistant can start to approach photographers about work. Tests or samples come into play here as well, as it is a sort of interviewing process. Both the photographer and the stylist can see if they work together without the pressure of a paying job and the presence of a client. Sometimes a photo assistant and styling assistant will bond and then carry that relationship on into their professional lives for years.

**Q. What do you like most and least about your job?**

**A.** My absolute favorite part of my job is how creative it is. I like going out into the world, finding things that could work for the project and bringing them in, putting them together, and making something. Working with a photographer can be so rewarding—he or she will groove on an idea or even an object, say a set of hand blown glasses, and we'll pursue various settings, surfaces, and situations of light. Then I'll be inspired by his or her ideas and start to come up with something that I never would have thought of on my own.

Perhaps the most challenging aspects to this job have to do with how many details there are to be dealt with in a short period of time. And then, if there are several projects in the works at once, keeping all the details together and the projects moving forward can be difficult.

This is a business full of large personalities. Managing egos while getting the job done and keeping one's own ego in line can be particularly challenging.

**Q. What advice would you give to high school students who are interested in this career?**

**A.** I would say classes and extracurricular activities in interior design, art, and photography would all be beneficial. A familiarity with architectural styles, general interior and furniture design, fabric and fiber content, and flower and plant identification is helpful. A general understanding of composition and color theory is important, as well as an understanding of basic photographic concepts. An ability to work with people and to be self-motivated, hard working, and flexible is critical, so any team activity (sports, etc.) would be a good way to learn those things. Knowing how to drive and access to a car is essential.

Look at catalogues and magazines for the kind of things they're interested in: cooking, home, fashion, etc. All the pictures in these two media have been styled.

Some financial understanding/budget/bookkeeping would be an enormous asset. Any small business seminar, computer training, Excel, word processing, Mac proficiency is a plus. Look for stylists' Web sites on the Internet. Also, hooking up with a stylist and observing a day on the job would definitely give students a good idea of what happens on a photo shoot or in preparation for it.

# Sports Photographers

## QUICK FACTS

**School Subjects**
Art
Physical education

**Personal Skills**
Artistic
Communication/ideas

**Work Environment**
Indoors and outdoors
Primarily multiple locations

**Minimum Education Level**
Some postsecondary training

**Salary Range**
$16,170 to $27,720 to
$59,890+

**Certification or Licensing**
Voluntary

**Outlook**
About as fast as the average

**DOT**
143

**GOE**
01.08.01

**NOC**
5221

**O*NET-SOC**
27-4021.00, 27-4021.01,
27-4021.02

## OVERVIEW

*Sports photographers* are specialists hired to shoot pictures of sporting events and athletes. They work for newspapers, magazines, and photo stock agencies to bring photos of events of all sizes (from a Little League game to the Olympics) to the pages of periodicals, the Internet, or other publications. Their pictures should clearly capture the movement, skill, and emotion of athletes. Approximately 122,000 photographers are employed in the United States; only a small percentage of these professionals specialize in sports photography.

## HISTORY

The Olympic Games are generally credited as being the first instance of organized sports. However, popular support for organized sports developed slowly. Prior to the 19th century, most sports were not officially organized; there were no official rules, competitions, or standards of play. During the 19th century, however, many sports underwent a transition from invented pastime to official sport. Rules governing play, the field of play, and competitions were agreed upon. The first modern track-and-field meet, for example, was held in England in 1825. Meanwhile, in the United States the English game of rugby evolved into American football. The first game was played between Rutgers and Princeton in 1869.

As sports grew in popularity, governing bodies and organizations were created to oversee the fair play of each sport. With this organization came public interest in the games. Gradually, coverage of sporting events on radio and in newspapers began to grow until sports quite literally became the national pastime for Americans. Newspapers assigned specialized reporters to capture sporting events to ensure complete and thorough coverage. Trained photographers were also sent to local and national events to capture pictures that evoked the blood, sweat, and tears of the sporting world's greatest athletes. With our current love affair with sports, photographers are now hired to take pictures of neighborhood tee-ball games to the World Series—and every pitch in between.

## THE JOB

Sports photographers are hired to shoot quality photos of sporting events, athletes, and crowds cheering on their home teams. Their work is published in newspapers, magazines, Web sites, books, and other sources.

Althouh they are usually trained as photographers, sports photographers must also have thorough knowledge of the sports they are assigned to shoot. Many sports photographers specialize in shooting one or two sports, such as soccer and hockey—both fast-moving, unpredictable sporting events to capture on film.

To be able to capture quick movements and subtle details on the athletes' faces, sports photographers must have good equipment. They need cameras with fast shutter speed abilities, tripods to hold cameras steady, and lenses of varying lengths to achieve appropriate depth of field for the intended image.

Sports photographers also need to be at the right place at the right time to get the best shots. Location is key when shooting sporting events. If photographers are too close to the action, they might get injured or, at the very least, interrupt play. If they are too far from the action, they will inevitably miss shots. They need to know where to position themselves to be able to capture the best moments of the game, such as a game-winning goal or a perfect header in soccer.

In addition to taking pictures, most sports photographers also spend some time developing film and printing photos. However, many now use digital cameras, which eliminate the need for separate developing and printing time. These photographers shoot a sporting event, then head back to their office to download the pictures onto a computer for printing or manipulation.

# REQUIREMENTS

## High School

While in high school, take photography classes and any other art classes that are offered. Even by studying painting, for example, you will learn about composition and balance, which are both important when shooting pictures. Physical education classes will introduce you to the rules of various sports, which will also come in handy when trying to capture images.

## Postsecondary Training

While not required, most sports photographers seek out college or art school degrees in photography to increase their skills and knowledge, build a portfolio, and make themselves stand out more to employers.

However, in this line of work, experience is more important than formal training. Only the well-practiced photographer is skilled enough to capture a soccer header or two athletes in mid-air fighting for a rebound. These shots require a lot of trial and error before getting the timing down, not to mention the right shutter speed, film, and aperture setting.

## Certification or Licensing

The Sports Photographers Association of America offers voluntary accreditation to sports photographers. Contact the association for more information. Additionally, the Professional Photographic Certification Commission offers a certification program for general photographers. Visit http://certifiedphotographer.com for more information.

## Other Requirements

In addition to knowing the ins and outs of photography, sports photographers need to know their game and photo subjects to be successful. For example, a football player who is known for a post-touchdown victory dance would make a good subject for a post-touchdown photo. Other players might be known for facial expressions, special moves, or other qualities that would be good to get on film. If possible, photographers should study individual athletes or teams for possible photo opportunities.

Because even the smallest detail could wreck or make a photo, sports photographers need to be thorough and patient when shooting pictures. They need to understand that they may need to take dozens of shots until they get the perfect image.

## Books to Read

Arndt, David Neil. *How to Shoot and Sell Sports Photography.* Buffalo, N.Y.: Amherst Media, 1999.
Skinner, Peter. *Sports Photography: How to Capture Action and Emotion.* New York: Allworth Press, 2007.
Steel, Andy. *The World's Top Photographers' Workshops: Sport & Action.* Hove, U.K.: Rotovision, 2008.
Timacheff, Serge, and David Karlins. *Digital Sports Photography: Take Winning Shots Every Time.* Hoboken, N.J.: Wiley, 2005.

## EXPLORING

You may want to join a school or club sports team to learn a sport in detail and build your skills. This will later help your career when sitting on the sidelines trying to position yourself to capture the best images.

Photography clubs are also a good idea to practice shooting and developing film and to meet other students with similar interests. Joining the school newspaper or yearbook staff is also a great way to gain experience in shooting sporting events. Most yearbooks and newspapers cover their team sports in detail, and photos are what make the stories stand out.

## EMPLOYERS

Sports photographers work for newspapers, sports magazines, Web sites, sports card companies, photo stock agencies, and wire services. Like many other types of photographers, sports photographers are sometimes self-employed and sell their photos to various sources for use in print and online publications.

## STARTING OUT

Beginning a career in photography can be an uphill battle. The equipment and materials are expensive, there is a lot of risk and competition for getting the right photo, and the pay may not be enough to support the photographer's craft. For this reason, many photographers hold other jobs in related fields, such as journalism or editing, and shoot pictures on the side.

Starting out, the photographer's main responsibilities should be to build a portfolio and make contacts in the area in which he or she would like to publish work. College internships with newspapers or magazines are a great way to accomplish both these tasks. An internship with a newspaper or sports magazine will introduce you to potential employers and allow you to build your body of work.

## ADVANCEMENT

Sports photographers advance by selling their work to highly respected publications (such as *Sports Illustrated* and *Sporting News*) and commanding more pay for their work. Some photographers become so well known for their work that they are requested by news organizations to shoot international or national sports events, such as the Olympics or the Super Bowl, year after year.

## EARNINGS

The earning potential for any photographer will vary depending on the shoot and where he or she is published. Typically, for sports photographers, the more important the sporting event, the higher the pay. Photographers shooting a college football game will earn less than those hired to shoot the Super Bowl.

The U.S. Department of Labor reports that photographers in general earned a median salary of $27,720 in 2007. The lowest paid 10 percent earned $16,170 or less, while the highest paid 10 percent earned $59,890 or more. During the same year, photographers working for newspapers, books, and other publishers earned an average of $40,070 annually.

Benefits for full-time workers include vacation and sick time, health, and sometimes dental, insurance, and pension or 401(k) accounts. Self-employed photographers must provide their own benefits. Some photographers may receive an allowance for equipment expenses.

## WORK ENVIRONMENT

Sports photographers work in an exciting environment that is constantly changing depending on their assignments. One day they may be working up in the bleachers of a hockey game, then the next day, they may be roaming the sidelines of a soccer match played in driving rain. One thing to note about their environment is the risk of injury. Because of their close proximity to the playing field, sports photographers have to be extremely careful when trying to get close enough for the best shots. While they may be concentrating deeply on capturing a great moment of a football game, they also must be able to quickly get themselves and their expensive equipment out of the way if a 275-pound linebacker suddenly heads their way.

In addition to shooting on location, sports photographers also spend time in darkrooms developing and printing film or at computers downloading pictures to instantly send to their employers.

## OUTLOOK

The U.S. Department of Labor predicts that employment of all photographers will grow about as fast as the average for all careers through 2016. Because competition for getting photos in top-selling newspapers and magazines can be tough, sports photographers who have a varied portfolio and are experienced with the latest digital camera equipment will find the most job opportunities.

## FOR MORE INFORMATION

*Visit the NPPA's Web site to see examples of award-winning photographs and to read resources geared directly toward students.*
**National Press Photographers Association (NPPA)**
3200 Croasdaile Drive, Suite 306
Durham, NC 27705-2588
Tel: 919-383-7246
Email: info@nppa.org
http://www.nppa.org

*For information about accreditation, contact*
**Sports Photographers Association of America**
c/o PMA-The Worldwide Community of Imaging Associations
3000 Picture Place
Jackson, MI 49201-8853
Tel: 800-762-9287
http://www.pmai.org/content.aspx?id=4772

*To access an online group of sports photographers, view images, and learn more about the career, visit the following Web site:*
**SportsShooter**
http://www.sportsshooter.com

# Index